SHAKESPEARE
IN THE THEATRE

Photo. Bassano.

Yours truly,
Wm Poel.

SHAKESPEARE
IN THE THEATRE

BY

WILLIAM POEL

FOUNDER AND DIRECTOR OF THE ELIZABETHAN
STAGE SOCIETY

BENJAMIN BLOM
New York

First published London, 1913
Reissued 1968,
by Benjamin Blom, Inc. Bx 10452

Library of Congress Catalog Card No. 67-31456

NOTE

THESE papers are reprinted from the *National Review*, the *Westminster Review*, the *Era*, and the *New Age*, by kind permission of the owners of the copyrights. The articles are collected in one volume, in the hope that they may be of use to those who are interested in the question of stage reform, more especially where it concerns the production of Shakespeare's plays.

W. P.

May, 1913.

ADDENDUM

An acknowledgement of permission to reprint should also have been made to the *Nation*, in which several of the most important of these papers originally appeared.

W. P.

Shakespeare in the Theatre

CONTENTS

I

THE STAGE OF SHAKESPEARE

II

THE PLAYS OF SHAKESPEARE

III

SOME STAGE VERSIONS

IV

THE NATIONAL THEATRE

I

THE STAGE OF SHAKESPEARE

THE ELIZABETHAN PLAYHOUSE
THE PLAYS AND THE PLAYERS

SHAKESPEARE IN THE THEATRE

I

THE STAGE OF SHAKESPEARE

THE ELIZABETHAN PLAYHOUSE.*

THE interdependence of Shakespeare's dramatic art with the form of theatre for which Shakespeare wrote his plays is seldom emphasized. The ordinary reader and the everyday critic have no historic knowledge of the Elizabethan playhouse; and however full the Elizabethan dramas may be of allusions to the contemporary stage, the bias of modern dramatic students is so opposed to any belief in the superiority of past methods of acting Shakespeare over modern ones, as to effectually bar any serious inquiry. A few sceptics have recognized dimly that a conjoint study of Shakespeare and the stage for which he wrote is possible; but they have not conducted their researches either seriously or impartially, and their conclusions have proved disputable and disappointing. With a very hazy perception of the connection between Elizabethan histrionic art and its literature, they have approached

* Part of a paper read before the Elizabethan Literary Society, November 1, 1893.

a comparison of the Elizabethan drama with the Elizabethan stage as they would a Chinese puzzle. They have read the plays in modern printed editions, they have seen them acted on the picture-stage, they have heard allusions made to old tapestry, rushes, and boards, and at once they have concluded that the dramatist found his theatre inadequate to his needs.

Now the first, and perhaps the strongest, evidence which can be adduced to disfavour this theory is the extreme difficulty—it might almost be said the impossibility—of discovering a single point of likeness between the modern idea of an Elizabethan representation of one of Shakespeare's plays, and the actual light in which it presented itself before the eyes of Elizabethan spectators. It is wasted labour to try to account for the perversities of the human intellect; but displays of unblushing ignorance have undoubtedly discouraged sober persons from pursuing an independent line of investigation, and have led many to deny the possibility of satisfactorily showing any intelligible connection between the Elizabethan drama and its contemporary exponents. Nowhere has a little knowledge proved more dangerous or more liable to misapplication, and nowhere has sure knowledge seemed more difficult of acquisition; yet it is obvious that investigators of the relations between the two subjects cannot command success unless they allow their theories to be formed by facts.

To those dilettante writers who believe that a poet's greatness consists in his power of emancipating himself from the limitations of time and space, it must sound something like impiety to describe Shakespeare's plays as in most cases compositions hastily written to fulfil the requirements of the moment and adapted to the wants of his theatre and the capabilities of his actors. But to persons of Mr. Ruskin's opinion this modified aspect should seem neither astonishing nor distressing; for they know that "it is a constant law that the greatest poets and historians live entirely in their own age, and the greatest fruits of their work are gathered out of their own age." Shakespeare and his companions were inspired by the prolific energies of their day. Their material was their own and their neighbours' experiences, and their plays were shaped to suit the theatre of the day and no other. It is therefore reasonable for the serious critic and historian to anticipate some increase of knowledge from a thorough examination of the Elizabethan theatre in close conjunction with the Elizabethan drama. Students who reject this method will always fail to realize the essential characteristic of one of the greatest ages of English dramatic poetry, while he who adopts it may confidently expect revelations of interest, not only to the playgoer, but to all who devote attention to dramatic literature. Above all things should it be borne in mind that the more the conditions of the Elizabethan theatre are studied, the better will it be perceived how workmanlike London's theatrical representations then were, and that they had nothing amateurish about them.

One of the chief fallacies in connection with the modern notion of the Elizabethan stage is that of its poverty in colour and setting through the absence of scenery—a notion that is at variance with every contemporary record of the theatre and of its puri-

tanical opponents, whose incessant taunts were,
" Behold the sumptuous theatre houses, a continual
monument of London's prodigality and folly." The
interior of an Elizabethan playhouse must have presented an unusually picturesque scene, with its mass
of colouring in the costume of the spectators ; while
the actors, moving, as it were, on the same plane as
the audience, and having attention so closely and
exclusively directed to them, were of necessity ap-
propriately and brilliantly attired. We hear much
from the superficial student about the " board being
hung up chalked with the words, ' This is a wood,'
when the action of the play took place in a forest."
But this is an impression apparently founded upon
Sir Philip Sidney's words in his "Apology of
Poetry," written about 1583 : " What child is there
that, coming to a play and seeing Thebes written in
great letters on an old door, doth believe that it is
Thebes ?" And whether these words were "chalked"
upon the outside door of the building admitting
to the auditorium, or whether they appeared exhibited to the eye of the audience on the stage-
door of the tiring-room is not made clear, but this
is certain, that there is no direct evidence yet forthcoming to prove that boards were ever used in any
of Shakespeare's dramas or in those of Ben Jonson ;
and, with some other dramatists, there is evidence
of the name of the play and its locality being shown
in writing, either by the prologue, or hung up on
one of the posts of the auditorium. Shakespeare
himself considered it to be the business of the
dramatist to describe the scene, and to call the attention of the audience to each change in locality, and
moreover he does this so skilfully as to make his

scenic descriptions appear as part of the natural
dialogue of the play. The naked action was assisted
by the poetry; and much that now seems superfluous in the descriptive passages was needed to
excite imagination. With reference to thi- question,
Halliwell Phillipps very justly remarks : "There
can be no doubt that Shakespeare, in the composition of most of his plays, could not have contemplated
the introduction of scenic accessories. It is fortunate that this should have been one of the conditions of his work, for otherwise many a speech of
power and beauty, many an effective situation, would
have been lost. All kinds of elaborate attempts at
stage illusion tend, moreover, to divert a careful
observance of the acting, while they are of no real
service to the imagination of the spectator, unless
the author renders them necessary for the full elucidation of his meaning. That Shakespeare himself
ridiculed the idea of a power to meet such a necessity, when he was writing for theatres like the
Curtain or Globe, is apparent from the opening
chorus to ' Henry V.' It is obvious that he wished
attention to be concentrated on the players and their
utterances, and that all surroundings, excepting
those which could be indicated by the rude .prop-
erties of the day, should be idealistic." The dramatist's disregard of time and place was justified by
the conditions of the stage, which left all to the
intellect ; a complete intellectual representation
being, in fact, a necessity, in the absence of meretri-
cious support. " The mind," writes John Addington
Symonds, " can contemplate the furthest just as
easily as more familiar objects, nor need it dread to
traverse the longest tract of years, the widest ex-

panse of space, in following the sequence of an action." In fact, the question of the advantage or disadvantage of scenery is well summed up by Collier, whose words are all the more impressive when it is borne in mind that his reasons are supported by an indisputable fact in the history of our dramatic literature. "Our old dramatists luxuriated in passages descriptive of natural or artificial beauty, because they knew their auditors would have nothing before their eyes to contradict the poetry ; the hangings of the stage made little pretension to be anything but covering for the walls, and the notion of the plays represented was taken from what was written by the poet, not from what was attempted by the painter. We owe to the absence of painted canvas many of the finest descriptive passages in Shakespeare, his contemporaries, and immediate followers. The introduction, we apprehend, gives the date to the commencement of the decline of our dramatic poetry." Shakespeare could not have failed to recognize that by employing the existing conventions of his stage he could the more readily bring the public to his point of view, since its thoughts were not being constantly diverted and distracted by those outward decorations and subordinate details which in our day so greatly obliterate the main object of dramatic work.

As the absence of theatrical machinery helped playwrights to be poets, so the capacity of actors stimulated literary genius to the creation of characters which the authors knew beforehand would be finely and intelligently rendered. Nor were the audiences in Shakespeare's time uncritical of the actor's art, and frequent allusions in the old plays show that they understood what " a clean action and good delivery" meant. To quote again from Mr. Addington Symonds, "attention was concentrated on the actors, with whose movements, boldly defined against a simple background, nothing interfered. The stage on which they played was narrow, projecting into the yard, surrounded on all sides by spectators. Their action was thus brought into prominent relief, placed close before the eye, deprived of all perspective. It acquired a special kind of realism which the vast distances and manifold artifices of our modern theatres have rendered unattainable. This was the realism of an actual event, at which the audience assisted ; not the realism of a scene in which the actor plays a somewhat subordinate part."

Noblemen used to maintain a musical establishment for the service of their chapels, and to this department of their household the actors belonged. When not required by their masters, these players strolled the country, calling themselves servants of the magnate whose pay they took and whose badge they wore. Thus Shakespeare's company first became known as "Lord Leicester's Servants," then as the Lord Chamberlain's, afterwards, in the reign of King James, as "The King's Company." And we can imagine the influence of the chapel upon the art of the theatre when we consider that choristers, who were taught to sing anthems and madrigals, would receive an excellent training for that rhythmical and musical modulation so indispensable to the delivery of blank verse. With regard to the boys who performed the female characters, it is specially to be noted that they were paid more than the ordinary actors, in consequence of the superior physical and vocal qualifications which were needed. That the boys were thoroughly successful in the delineation of women's parts we learn from the Puritans, and from the insistence that those boys impressed for Queen Elizabeth's chapel should not only be skilled in the art of minstrelsy, but also be handsome and shapely, which seems to point to the theatrical use that would be made of them.   To this end, power was given to the Queen's choirmaster to impress boys from any chapel in the United Kingdom, St. Paul's only excepted. A contemporary play has the following allusion to a boy actor : " Afore Heaven it is a sweet-faced child.   Methinks he would show well in woman's attire.   I'll help thee to three crowns a week for him, an she can act well."

Referring once more to the construction of the theatres, it is important to note that they differed most from modern playhouses in their size ; not so much, perhaps, in the size of the stage as in the dimensions of the auditorium.   The building was so made that the remotest spectator could hardly have been distant more than a dozen yards, or thereabouts, from the front of the stage.   The whole auditory were thus within a hearing distance that conveyed the faintest modulation of the performer's voice, and at the same time demanded no exaggerated effort in the more sonorous utterances.   Especially would such a building be well adapted for the skilled and rapid delivery for which Elizabethan players were famous.   Added to this, every lineament of the actor's countenance would have been visible without telescopic aid.   It was for such a theatre that Shakespeare wrote, says Mr. Halliwell Phillips, "one wherein an actor of genius could satisfactorily develop to every one of the audience not merely the written, but the unwritten words of the drama, those latter which are expressed by gesture or by the subtle language of the face and eye. There is much of the unrecorded belonging to the pages of Shakespeare that requires to be elicited in action, and no little of that much which can only be effectively rendered under conditions similar to those which prevailed at the opening of the Globe."

Suitable to the construction of the Elizabethan theatre was the construction of the Elizabethan play, the most noticeable feature of which was the absence of division into scenes and acts. For even when a new act and scene are marked in the old quartos and folios, they are probably only printer's divisions, and we find the text often continuing the story as though the characters had not left the stage. Not that it is to be inferred that no pauses were made during the representation of the play, especially at the cheaper and more popular houses, where jigs and musical interludes were among the staple attractions. But judging from the following words put into Burbage's mouth by Webster in his induction to "The Malcontent" (a play that originally had been written for the Fortune theatre), we may gather that at the Globe it was not usual to have musical intervals.

"*W. Sly:* What are your additions?

"*D. Burb.:* Sooth, not greatly needful, only as your sallet to your great feast, to entertain a little more time, and to abridge the not received custom of music in our theatre."

Nor is it likely Shakespeare would have approved

of any interruptions to the dramatic movement of his plays when once it had begun. He made very sparing use of the chorus, and avoided both prologue and epilogue when possible.

There is, in this same induction by Webster, some dialogue that throws light also upon the estimation in which Shakespeare and his fellow actors regarded their calling and its duties and responsibilities, and is worth quoting:

" *W. Sly:* And I say again, the play is bitter.

"*D. Burb.:* Sir, you are like a patron that, presenting a poor scholar to a benifice, enjoins him not to rail against anything that stands within compass of his patron's folly. Why should we not enjoy the antient freedom of poesy? Shall we protest to the ladies that their painting makes them angels? or to my young gallant, that his expence in the brothel shall gain him reputation? No, sir; such vices as stand not accountable to law should be cured as men heal tetters, by casting ink upon them."

Above all things, may it be acknowledged that if the Fortune theatre, the great rival playhouse to the Globe, was the most successful and prosperous financially, the Lord Chamberlain's troupe appealed, through Shakespeare, to the highest faculties of the audience, and showed in their performances a certain unity of moral and artistic tone.

The Plays and the Players.*

An Englishman visiting Venice about 1605 wrote in a letter from that city: "I was at one of their

---

* *The National Review*, August, 1890.

playhouses where I saw a comedy acted. The house is very beggarly and base in comparison with our stately playhouses in England, neither can the actors compare with us for apparel, shows, and music." This opinion is confirmed by Busino, who has left an account of his visit to the Fortune playhouse in 1617, where he observed a crowd of nobility " listening as silently and soberly as possible." And Thomas Heywood the dramatist, not later than 1612, affirms that the English stage is " an ornament to the city which strangers of all nations repairing hither report of in their countries, beholding them here with some admiration, for what variety of entertainment can there be in any city of Christendom more than in London?" In fact, the English people at this time, like the Greeks and Romans before them, were lovers of the theatre and of tragic spectacles. Leonard Digges, who was an eye-witness, has left on record the impression made upon the spectators by a representation of one of Shakespeare's tragedies:

> " So have I seen when Cæsar would appear,
>   And on the stage at half-sword parley were
>   Brutus and Cassius. Oh ! how the audience
>   Were ravished, with what wonder they went thence !"

But plays as perfect in design as " Julius Cæsar," " Othello," and " Macbeth " were the exception, not the rule, upon the Elizabethan stage. They were the outcome of nearly twenty years' experiment in play-writing, a period during which Shakespeare mastered his art and schooled his audience to appreciate the serious unmixed with the ludicrous. When he first wrote for the stage, plays needed to have in them all that the taste of the day demanded in the way of comic interlude and music. A dramatic representation was a continuous performance given without pause from beginning to end, and the dramatists, in compliance with the custom, used the double story, so often to be found in the plays of the time, in order that the movement should be continued uninterruptedly. The characters in each story appeared on the stage in alternate scenes, with every now and then a full scene in which all the characters appeared together. Ben Jonson condemned this form of play. He ridiculed the use of short scenes, and the bringing on to the stage of the characters in pairs. Yet he himself found it necessary to conform to the requirements of the day, as is shown in his first two comedies, written to be acted without pause from beginning to end. Later on he adopted the Terentian method of construction, that of dividing the plays into acts and making each act a complete episode in itself; and in his dedication prefixed to the play of " The Fox," he claims to have laboured " to reduce not only the ancient forms, but manners of the scene." There can be no doubt, therefore, that Ben Jonson disliked Shakespeare's tolerance of the hybrid class of play then in vogue. Yet Shakespeare, if he thought it was not possible to work to the satisfaction of his audience according to the rules and examples of the ancients, none the less strove to put limits to the irregularities of his contemporaries. At the Universities scholars regarded his plays as compositions that were written for the public stage and therefore of no intrinsic value; while Londoners must have looked upon them as representations of actual life when compared with the formless dramas they were accustomed to see He desired unity of fable with variety of movement, and endeavoured to abolish the use of impromptu dialogue by writing his own interludes and making them part of the play. Shakespeare wished to satisfy his audience and himself at the same time ; and by the force of his dramatic genius he succeeded where others failed, and wrote plays which, if unsuitable for the modern stage, are still being acted.

About two-thirds of the plays which were acted at the Elizabethan and Jacobean theatres are now lost to us ; and this dramatic literature must have been of unusual excellence, unless we are to suppose that the law of the survival of the fittest may be applied to the lives of plays. From the names of extinct dramas, accessible to us in such places as Henslowe's "Diary" or the Stationers' Registers, it may be inferred that the groundwork of many of them consisted either of political or purely social and domestic topics. Domestic tragedy was one of the most popular forms of the drama. In fact the dramatists, in most instances, took the material for their plays from their own and their neighbours' experiences, and all that was uppermost in men's minds was laid hold of by them, and brought upon the stage with only a little transparent concealment. The topical Elizabethan drama, in the plays which have come down to us, viewed from a purely historical standpoint, is a very accurate though not very flattering embodiment of middle-class society in London in the sixteenth century. From it we learn the dangers incurred by the presence of a large class of riotous idlers, discharged soldiers and sailors, over whom the authorities exercised little control; we are given striking descriptions of the London "roughs"; of these "swagging, swearing, drunken, desperate Dicks, that have the stab readier in their hands than a penny in their purses." We read, too, of the games that children played in the streets; of the assembling of the men of fashion and business in St. Paul's; and of the dense crowding of the neighbouring streets at the dinner-hour, when the throng left the cathedral. The conversation that the characters indulge in, apart from the immediate plot, invariably relates to current events. In a play written about the time of the Irish rebellion, one of the characters talks about Ireland in a way that might apply to recent days :

> " The land gives good increase
> Of every blessing for the use of man,
> And 'tis great pity the inhabitants
> Will not be civil and live under law."

Uninteresting and unsavoury as some of the details of the Elizabethan domestic tragedies are, they were often used with an avowedly moral aim, and they had, according to many contemporary accounts, the most salutary effect on evil-doers.* It was not more than forty years after Shakespeare's death that Richard Flecknoe, in his "Discourse of the English Stage," comments upon the altered character of the drama :

" Now for the difference betwixt our Theatres and those of former times ; they were but plain and simple, with no other scenes nor decorations of the stage, but only old Tapestry, and the

---

* See "The Topical Side of the Elizabethan Drama" in the Transactions of the New Shakspere Society, 1887.

Stage strewed with Rushes, whereas ours for cost and ornament are arrived at the height of Magnificence, but that which makes our Stage the better, makes our Playes the worse, perhaps through striving now to make them more for sight than hearing, whence that solid joy of the interior is lost, and that benefit which men formerly received from Playes, from which they seldom or never went away but far better and wiser than when they came."

The short space of time—two hours and a half—in which an Elizabethan play was acted in Shakespeare's time, has excited much discussion among commentators. It can hardly be doubted that the dialogue, which often exceeds two thousand lines, was all spoken on the stage, for none of the dramatists wrote with a view to publication, and few of the plays were printed from the author's manuscript. This fact points to the employment of a skilled and rapid delivery on the part of the actor. Artists of the French school, whose voices are highly trained and capable of a varied and subtle modulation, will run through a speech of fifty lines with the utmost ease and rapidity; and there is good reason to suppose that the blank verse of the Elizabethan dramatists was spoken "trippingly on the tongue." And then only a few of the plays which were written for the public stage were divided into acts; and even in the case of a five act drama it was not thought necessary to mark each division with an interval, since the jigs and interludes were reserved for the end of the play. So with an efficient elocution and no "waits," the Elizabethan actors would have got through one-half of a play before our modern actors could cover a third. Even Ben Jonson, while disliking the form of the Elizabethan drama, recognized the advantage to the dramatist of simplicity in the

2

method of representation. He alludes, with not a little contempt, to Inigo Jones's costly settings of the masque at the court of King James.

> " A wooden dagger is a dagger of wood,
>   Nor gold nor ivory haft can make it good . . .
>   Or to make boards to speak !   There is a task !
>   Painting and carpentry are the soul of masque.
>   Pack with your pedling poetry to the Stage.
>   This is the money-got mechanic age !"

If a theatre were established in this country for the performance of Shakespeare's plays with the simplicity and rapidity with which they were acted in his time, it might limit the endless experiments, mutilations, and profitless discussions that every revival occasions. " To read a play," said Robert Louis Stevenson, " is a knack, the fruit of much knowledge and some imagination, comparable to that of reading score "; the reader is apt to miss the proper point of view. In omitting one-third of the play every time Shakespeare is acted, the most appropriate scenes for representation may not always be chosen. But were the entire play acted occasionally, the author's point of view could not fail to declare itself. It is interesting to note that Germany, always to the fore in Shakespearian matters, has obtained in Baron Perfall, the director of the Royal Court Theatre in Munich, an advocate for the performance of Shakespeare's plays as they were originally acted.

The Elizabethan dramatists, as a rule, deprecated the printing of their plays. They regretted that " scenes invented merely to be spoken should be inforcively published to be read." Elocution was

to the playwrights an all-important consideration.
They acknowledge that the success of their labours
" lay much in the actor's voice"; that he must speak
well, "though he understand not what," for if the
actor had not "a facility and natural dexterity in
his delivery, it must needs sound harsh to the
auditor, and procure his distaste and displeasure."
A good tragedy, in Ben Jonson's opinion, "must
have truth of argument, dignity of persons, gravity
and height of elocution "; " words," he says, " should
be chosen that have their sound ample, the composition full, the absolution plenteous, and poured out
all grave, sinewy, and strong."   And Thomas Heywood, in 1612, thus writes in defence of the actor's
art : " Tully, in his booke, ' Ad Caium Herennium,'
requires five things in an orator—invention, disposition, eloqution, memory, and pronuntiation ; yet all
are imperfect without the sixt, which is action : for
be his invention never so fluent and exquisite, his
disposition and order never so composed and formall,
his eloquence and elaborate phrases never so materiall
and pithy, his memory never so ferme and retentive,
his pronuntiation never so musical and plausive ;
yet without a comely and elegant gesture, a gratious
and a bewitching kinde of action, a natural and
familiar motion of the head, the hand, the body, and
a moderate and fit countenance suitable to all the
rest, I hold all the rest as nothing.   A delivery and
sweet action is the glosse and beauty of any discourse
that belongs to a scholler ; and this is the action be-
hoovefull in any that professe this quality, not to use
any impudent or forced motion in any part of the
body, nor rough or other violent gesture, nor, on the
contrary, to stand like a stiffe starcht man, but to

qualifie everything according to the nature of the person personated: for in overacting trickes, and toyling too much in the anticke habit of humors, men of the ripest desert, greatest opinions, and best reputations may breake into the most violent absurdities.   I take not upon me to teach, but to advise ; for it becomes my juniority rather to be pupil'd my selfe than to instruct others."

Shakespeare, also, though not so great an actor as he was a dramatist, knew as well what was needed for the art of the one as of the other, and perhaps thought even more about the acting because he had the less genius for it.   There are some descriptive passages in his plays which show that he visualized the characters he created and gave them gestures which were appropriate to their personalities.

If the actors were fortunate in having poets such as Shakespeare, Jonson, and Heywood, not only to write for them, but also to instruct them, the poets were no less fortunate in their actors.   Of Burbage, we are told that he had all the parts of an excellent orator, animating his words with his speech, and his speech with action, so that his auditors were "never more delighted than when he spoke, nor more sorry than when he held his peace ; yet even then he was an excellent actor still, never failing in his part when he had done speaking, but with his looks and gesture maintaining it still unto the height."   We learn that he was small in stature ; that every thought and mood could be understood from his face ; and that because of his gifts he was "only worthy to come on the stage," and because of his honesty "he was more worthy than to come on."   So great was Burbage's popularity that London received the news

of his death, which occurred within a few days of
that of the Queen, King James's Consort, with
a greater manifestation of grief than they bestowed
on the lady.   Perhaps Shakespeare was thinking of
Burbage's unusual ability when he wrote the following lines :

> " The eyes of men
> After a well-grac'd actor leaves the stage
> Are idly bent on him that enters next,
> Thinking his prattle to be tedious."

Dick Robinson was an actor of women's parts.
Ben Jonson has left on record that he could dress
better than forty women, and, in the disguise of a
lawyer's wife, he could convulse a supper party with
merriment.   Acting so realistic as his stirred the
resentment of the Puritans.   Stephen Gosson writes :
" Which way, I beseech you, shall they be excused
that put on, not the apparel only, but the gate, the
gestures, the voice, the passions of a woman."
Nathan Field was the son of a minister, who was
one of the earliest as well as one of the bitterest
enemies of theatrical performances.   While one of
the Royal Chapel boys, Field distinguished himself
in Ben Jonson's comedy, " Cynthia's Revels," acted
entirely by children.   Afterwards Field became a
member of Shakespeare's company, and, like him,
an author.   When Burbage died, Field was his suc-
cessor in the part of the Moor.   It is said that as he
was naturally of a jealous disposition, the character
suited him, and his impersonation of it became famed
as " the true Othello of the poet."   Many particulars
have come down to us of the clown, Kemp.   His
popularity with his audiences cannot be disputed.
" Clowns," writes a dramatic author in 1597, " have

been thrust into plays by the head and shoulders ever since Kemp could make a scurvy face. . . . If thou canst but draw thy mouth awry, lay thy leg over thy staff, saw a piece of cheese asunder with thy dagger, lap up drink on the earth, I warrant thee they'll all laugh mightily." It was by tricks such as these that Kemp won the good opinion "of the understanding gentlemen of the ground"; but Shakespeare was not in favour of fooling. Kemp, moreover, loved to extemporize, and Shakespeare wished to abolish a custom fatal to dramatic unity. He preferred to write the clown's part himself, and desired that no more should be spoken than was set down by the author. The interference with the clown's privilege, openly advocated by Shakespeare in a well-known passage of "Hamlet," probably led to Kemp's temporary retirement from the company. Kemp loved notoriety and money. His morris dance to Norwich and journeys to France and Italy were but gambling speculations, he undertaking to be back in a certain time, and laying wagers with large odds in his favour to that effect.

The prosperity of the actor caused many to adopt the calling. His vocation, we are told, was the most excellent one in the world for money, and therefore players grew as plentifully "as spawn of frogs in March." It was open to the actor to buy shares in his theatre, and he could, by becoming a shareholder, attain the position of owner, and would, in Shakespeare's theatre, as one of the King's players, be provided from the royal wardrobe "with a cloak of bastard-scarlet and crimson velvet for the cape." He could also term himself "gentleman," a rank he

was allowed to assume, and which he was very glad
to adopt in defiance of the enemies of theatrical performances, who constantly taunted him, in the words
of the old statute, with being "a rogue and a vaga-
bond."   The popularity of the stage as a profession
excited the envy of scholars and lawyers.   They
taunted the actor with his vanity in believing that
his fame would descend to posterity.   They blamed
the public for affording these "glorious vagabonds"
means to ride through the "gazing streets" in satin
clothes attended by their pages, and for enabling
those who had done no more than "mouth words
that better wits had framed" to purchase lands and
possess country houses.   The actor retaliated by
deriding the scholar's poverty and ridiculing the
lawyer's use of bad Latin.   They contended that
it was better "to make a fool of the world than
to be fooled of the world as you scholars are."
There is an anecdote related of Nathan Field
which shows that actors did not underrate their
own importance.

"Nathan Field, the player, being in company with
a certain nobleman who was distantly related to
him, the latter asked the reason why they spelt
their names differently, the nobleman's family spel-
ing it 'Feild,' and the player spelling it 'Field'?   'I
cannot tell,' answered the player, 'except it be that
my branch of the family were the first that knew to
spell.'"   It would hardly have been agreeable to
this tragedian to learn that he and his fellows,
Shakespeare and Burbage, were "writ down" by
the Master of His Majesty's Revels as "players,
jugglers, and such kind of creatures"; nor would
Ben Jonson have felt flattered by the candid con-

fession of an admirer who "could not understand how a poet could have so much principle."

Most of the leading actors in Shakespeare's theatre had their apprentices. A stage aspirant was often called upon to appear before the leading members of the company, and to give some proof of his talent. No little importance was attached to the youth's appearance, to his command of facial expression, and to the sufficiency of his voice. If the young man's talent lay in the direction of comedy, Kemp might address him after this manner : "Methinks you should belong to my tuition, and your face, methinks, would be good for a foolish mayor, or a foolish justice of peace." Not seldom the efforts of novices to copy nature excited the derision of experts. Kemp, as a character in a play— "The Return from Parnassus"acted about 1601—says to Burbage: "It is a good sport in a part to see them never speak but at the end of the stage, just as though, in walking with a fellow, we should never speak but at a stile, a gate, or a ditch, where a man can go no further." Besides having a good memory, an actor needed the gift of studying quickly. It is not generally known that the expression "to sleep on a part," still in use among actors, was current in Shakespeare's day ; but we read in an old play of an actor, whose memory had failed him while acting his part, blaming the negligence of the man in charge of the stage: "It is all along of you. I could not get my part a night or two before to sleep upon it." The prompter, or "book-holder," as he was more often called, was not an unnecessary person on a "new day," the first performance of a new play. He would have received many a warning to "hold the book well, that we be not *non plus* in the latter end of the play." And Ben Jonson has given an amusing description of an additional supervision on the part of the author that was not of the actor's seeking, "to have his presence in the tiring-house, to prompt us aloud, stamp at the bookholder, swear for our properties, curse the poor tireman, rail the music out of tune, and sweat for every venal trespass we commit." The members of a theatrical company being limited in number, it was often necessary for the impersonators of kings and heroes to represent very inferior characters in the same play, a circumstance to the advantage of the dramatist, who could thus obtain capable exponents for the parts of messengers and attendants, and was able, therefore, to "write up" these parts without fear of the author's lines being mangled by incompetence, or made ridiculous by false pretension. Actors who doubled their parts wore the double cloak—a cloak that might be worn on either side. A turned cloak, with a false beard and a black or yellow peruke, supplied a ready, if not effectual, disguise.

Although the theatres were prosperous, their existence was often imperilled by the action of the city magnates, who forbad the acting of plays within their own jurisdiction. They viewed with annoyance the crowds that came from north and south to bring money to the playhouses, and they disliked the inducements these afforded to their sons and apprentices to neglect their occupations. No opportunity was lost by the Corporation of urging the Sovereign to abolish the theatres. The Puritans, also, if not influential at Court, were still potent in affecting public opinion against stage-plays, in the pulpit and by means of the Press; while playwrights were even more violently attacked by them than were the actors. The sonorous and majestic verse of the Elizabethan poets, that has become the pride of our country, appeared in the eyes of the "godly" but as an invention of Satan to entice the unwary into his "chapel."

"Because the sweete numbers of Poetrie flowing in verse do wōderfully tickle the hearers eares, the devill hath tyed this to most of our playes, that whatsoever he would have sticke fast to our soules might slippe down in sugar by this intisement; for that which delighteth never troubleth our swallow. Thus when any matter of love is interlarded, though the thinge it selfe bee able to allure us, yet it is so sette out with sweetnes of wordes fitness of Epithites, with Metaphors, Alegories, Hyperboles, Amphibologies, Similitudes : with Phrases so pickt, so pure, so proper ; with action so smothe, so lively, so wantō, that the poyson creeping on secretly without griefe chookes us at last and hurleth us downe in a dead sleepe."

This vigorous opposition to the stage had its advantage. It kept managers alive to their responsibilities, and obliged them to maintain a high standard of work. The poets were called upon to justify the existence of playhouses, and to defend their own reputations, and in this they were triumphant. They showed that playwrights had followed the advice of Cicero, and could create a drama which was "the schoolmistress of life, the looking-glass of manners, and the image of truth." They contended that in the theatre men were shown, as in a mirror, "their faults though ne'er so small." Of Shakespeare's comedies it was said, they are "so framed to the life, that they serve for the most common commentaries of all the actions of

our lives, and all such dull and heavy-witted world-
ings, as were never capable of the wit of a comedy,
coming by report of them to his representations
have found that wit there that they never found in
themselves, and have parted better-witted than they
came." Thomas Heywood contended that plays had
made "the ignorant more apprehensive, taught the
unlearned the knowledge of many famous histories,
instructed such as cannot read in the discovery of
all our English Chronicles, and what man have you
now of that weak capacity that cannot discourse of
any notable thing recorded, even from William the
Conqueror; nay, from the landing of Brute until this
day." Perhaps it was well for the public of Shakespeare's day that it attached an educational value
to the theatre, and consciously adopted an attitude
of diffidence towards the labours of the dramatist.
He was left free to teach as well as to amuse. If
the amusement consisted in putting into the mouths
of the clowns "unsavoury morsels of unseemly
sentences," the teaching consisted in making folly
appear ridiculous and vice odious. So long as the
dramatists were not hampered by demands from the
audience to have its social, political, or æsthetic
fancies humoured, and from the actor to have his
egotism flattered, the drama flourished as an art as
well as a business. But when managers began to consider the whims of their patrons, when the King's
Players petitioned the People's Parliament for leave
to continue their vocation because "they will not
entertain any comedian that shall speak his part in a
tone as if he did it in derision of some of the pious,"
then the theatre ceased to be a looking-glass that
could image life truthfully. Indeed, it cannot be

doubted that if ever the drama shall again enlist the best talent of the time in its service it will be when the nation becomes conscious of the power of the stage, which is capable, as Bacon says, "of no small influence, both of discipline and corruption."

II

THE PLAYS OF SHAKESPEARE

SOME MISTAKES OF THE EDITORS.
SOME MISTAKES OF THE ACTORS.
THE CHARACTER OF LADY MACBETH.
SHAKESPEARE'S JEW AND MARLOWE'S
CHRISTIANS.
THE AUTHORS OF "KING HENRY THE
EIGHTH."
"TROILUS AND CRESSIDA."

II

THE PLAYS OF SHAKESPEARE*

NEITHER in the theatre nor on the printed page can
it be said that Shakespeare's dramas to-day reflect
the form of his art or the thought of his age.   The
versions acted on the stage are unlike those read in
the study, and all are dissimilar to the "authentic
copies."   In order to understand the cause of these
discrepancies it is necessary to trace their origin and
history.

SOME MISTAKES OF THE EDITORS

A number of Shakespeare's plays were published
during his lifetime, the first, "The Comedy of
Errors," appearing in 1595, and the last one,
"Pericles," in 1609.   Some of these plays went
through several editions, and the text of four of
them, in their first edition, was extremely faulty,
but the second editions of "Romeo and Juliet" and
of "Hamlet" were probably printed direct from the
author's manuscripts.

The special features of these early quartos are :

1. The title-pages, which indicate what in Shakespeare's time were the popular incidents and
characters in each play.

* The first three articles of this chapter appeared in *The Nation*,
March, 1912.

2. The unbroken continuity of the story, the plays having no divisions to suggest where pauses were made, if any, during the representation.

3. Some descriptive stage-directions which do not reappear in subsequent editions, and which in all probability are authentic evidence of the action as it was then seen on the stage.

These quartos are the only playbooks existing to-day which can show Shakespeare's constructive art as a dramatist, and it will be necessary to refer to them from time to time.

Seven years after his death, Shakespeare's fellow-actors, Heminge and Condell, collected all his dramas, and, with the help of some booksellers, published them in one volume in what is known as the first folio (1623). These "trifles," as the editors called them, were dedicated to two noblemen in the confidence that this tribute would help to keep the author's memory alive, and the reader is invited to purchase the book because the plays had found favour on the stage where they were first tried and "stood out all appeales." There is, besides, some anxiety shown by the editors lest the publication of the volume should detract from the author's fame as a dramatist, for the reader is urged to read the plays "againe and againe," if he does not like them, or in other words, if he does not understand them. Now, in this first folio, Heminge and Condell began marking divisions for intervals in the plays. This was an innovation, probably suggested to them by the book-sellers at the instigation of Ben Jonson. Fortunately, the editors left their task unfinished, finding, perhaps, that these divisions were unsuitable interpolations.

In 1709 there came a new phase in the history of Shakespearian Bibliography when Rowe, the poet-dramatist, at the suggestion of his bookseller, who believed that "none but a poet should presume to meddle with a poet," undertook to present to the world a new edition of Shakespeare's plays, in which the player-dramatist was for the first time to be brought within the fraternity of academicians. His works were to be edited on similar lines to those of the poets of Rowe's time, with the appendage of a life and a recommendatory preface. The contrast between this preface and that of Heminge and Condell is characteristic. To Rowe it is "a great wonder" that Shakespeare should have advanced dramatic poetry as far as he did ; and, since he wrote "under a mere light of nature," and was never acquainted with Aristotle's precepts, it would be hard to "judge him by a law he knew nothing of." With Rowe, also, the "fable" comes first for criticism, because even if it is not the most difficult or beautiful part of the play, it is the most important ; yet he contends that in this art Shakespeare has "no mastery or strength." In accordance with academic notions, Rowe completes the work begun by Heminge and Condell, and divides all the plays into acts and scenes ; cutting up the text, as it is said, on "rational principles."* But Rowe's divisions are both misplaced and unauthorized ; and even his text is faulty through being printed from the fourth edition of the first folio, the latest one and the least accurate.

Pope follows Rowe as editor in 1723, and upholds the authority of the early copies, which, as he says with truth, "hold the place of the originals, and are

* Sir Sidney Lee, " Dictionary of National Biography."

the only materials left to repair the deficiencies, or restore the corrupted sense of the author." Pope's study of the "originals," however, confirms him in Rowe's opinion that Heminge and Condell were ignorant men, both as editors and actors. It was—

"Ben Jonson, getting possession of the stage, brought critical learning into vogue: and that this was not done without difficulty may appear from those frequent lessons (and indeed almost declamations) which he was forced to prefix to his first plays, and put into the mouth of his actors. . . . Till then, our authors had no thoughts of writing on the model of the ancients: their tragedies were only histories in dialogue: and their comedies followed the thread of any novel as they found it no less implicitly than if it had been true history."

Pope also remarks that "players have ever had a standard to themselves upon other principles than those of Aristotle," and Shakespeare's "wrong judgment as a poet" must be ascribed to his "right judgment as a player." It is evident, then, that Pope, like Rowe, had nothing favourable to say about Shakespeare's art in the management of his "fable," and if Heminge and Condell put in some act and scene divisions, "often where there is no pause in the action," Pope marks a change of scene at every removal of place, "which is more necessary in this author than in any other, because he shifts them more frequently."

It was said of Pope's edition that he had rejected whatever he disliked, and thought more of amputation than cure. In the controversy which followed, Pope found his match in Theobald. This critic points out in his preface (1726) that an editor should be well versed in the history and manners of his author's age, "if he aim at doing him service." But Theobald, like Rowe, fails to understand Shake-

speare's dramatic art, and compares him with a
"corrupt classic" for whom classical remedies are
necessary. Fortunately, Theobald confines his attention entirely to textual emendations, and, unlike
Pope, he does not tamper with the text in order to
make Shakespeare "speak better than the old copies
have done." Johnson, in spite of his censure,
honoured Theobald by borrowing largely from his
labours in his own edition.

Warburton (1747) defends Pope, and shrewdly
remarks that Shakespeare's works "when they
escaped the players did not fall into much better
hands when they came amongst printers and book-
sellers," adding, "the truth is Shakespeare's condition was yet but ill-understood." But Warburton
is wanting in historical knowledge when he writes,
"The stubborn nonsense, with which he was in-
crusted, occasioned his lying long neglected amongst
the common lumber of the stage." In fact, Warburton abuses Rowe's editing, yet none the less adopts
his tone in disparaging "those impurities," the
original copies.

Dr. Johnson (1765) brings vigour and common sense
to bear upon his editorial labours, without, however,
betraying special sympathy with the poet's achieve-
ments, or any subtle comprehension of his art as a
dramatist. But Johnson never forgets that Shakespeare wrote plays and not poems, and that he sold
them to actors and not printers. His criticisms are
those of a playgoer writing of plays, as if he had
seen them acted at the theatre. At the same time
he follows Rowe's lead in saying that Shakespeare's
plots are so loosely constructed that not one play
would now "be heard to the conclusion," and

similarly with Rowe, he generalizes as to the text being vitiated " by the blunders of the penman, or changed by the affectation of the players." About the division into acts and scenes, he writes :

" I have preserved the common distribution of the plays into acts, though I believe it to be in almost all the plays void of authority. Some of those which are divided in the later editions have no division in the first folio, and some that are divided in the folio have no division in the preceding copies. The settled mode of the theatre requires four intervals in the play, but few if any of our author's compositions can be properly distributed in that manner. An act is so much of the drama as passes without intervention of time or change of place. A pause makes a new act. In every real and therefore in every imitative action, the intervals may be more or fewer, the restriction of five acts being accidental and arbitrary. This Shakespeare knew, and this he practised ; his plays were written, and at first printed in one un-broken continuity, and ought now to be exhibited with short pauses, interposed as often as the scene is changed, or any con-siderable time is required to pass. This method would at once quell a thousand absurdities."

Something must be said later on about the " short pauses." There is wisdom as well as humour in Johnson's observation: " Let him who desires to feel the highest pleasure that the drama can give read every play from the first scene to the last with utter negligence of all his commentators."

To Steevens belongs the credit of being the first to collect and reprint (1766) in one volume the original quartos, of which a revised and completed edition is much needed. " Many of the quartos," he writes, " as our own printers assure me, were far from being unskilfully executed, and some of them were much more correctly printed than the folio." With regard to Shakespeare's text, he observes: " To make his meaning intelligible to his audience seems to have been his only care, and with the ease of conversation he has adopted its incorrectness." In fact, Steevens thinks that Shakespeare, of all the writers of his day, was the most ungrammatical.

Capell (1768) is perhaps the least dogmatic of all the eighteenth-century editors, and the most cautious in his judgment, when he remarks: "Generally speaking, the more distant a new edition is from its original, the more it abounds in faults which is done by destroying all marks of peculiarity and notes of time." And in another passage: "That division of scenes which Jonson seems to have attempted, and upon which the French stage prides itself, Shakespeare does not appear to have any idea of." In a note he adds: "The current editions are divided in such a manner that nothing like a rule can be collected from any of them." Unfortunately, like all the other editors, Capell believes it necessary to divide Shakespeare's plays into acts and scenes.

With Malone (1790) Shakespearian criticism enters upon a new phase—the historical one—when research and evidence take precedence of conjecture. What he says of the first editors of his century remains as true to-day as it was when written—"that the men never looked behind them, but considered their own era and their own phraseology as the standard of perfection."

Malone, moreover, observes that the two chief duties of an editor are to show the genuine text of an author and to explain his obscurities. This, it must be admitted, is the view taken by all his contemporaries; and yet dramas are not poems any more than words are deeds. And while Malone spares no pains to amend a corrupt text in the hope of arriving at verbal accuracy, he has little scruple about marring Shakespeare's scheme of action. "All the stage-directions," he writes, "throughout this work I have considered as wholly in my power, and have regulated them in the best manner I could." To do this is to run counter to an editor's province and duty; for a dramatist to know that his text is correct affords him small consolation if his story has been misunderstood and mutilated. It is doubtful whether scholars who insist on editing Shakespeare's plays as if they were anything or everything but drama have any just appreciation of the work they undertake. When Dr. Johnson contends that Shakespeare was "read, admired, and imitated while he was yet deformed," he is indirectly praising deformity. All the eighteenth-century editors blame Shakespeare for the management of his "fable," and attribute it to his ignorance, while many modern editors altogether overlook his art of making a play. The late Dr. Furnivall's introduction to the "Leopold Shakespeare," which has been deservedly and universally praised, has yet one vital defect as dramatic criticism—his comments apply to the art of a novelist, not to that of a playwright.

The arguments brought forward in the Bacon-Shakespeare controversy are a striking illustration of this imperfect knowledge. While the Baconians pride themselves on discovering a similarity in the phraseology or philosophical sentiments of the two writers, they forget that Shakespeare was pre-eminent in the writing of drama—an art which is as difficult to master as that of a painter or a musician, and in which the hand of an amateur can be as easily detected ; an art for which Bacon showed no aptitude, and for which he had had no training. A novelist who describes characters vividly was once asked why she seldom made them talk. Her answer was : " I have little talent for writing dialogue ; when my characters speak they often cease to be the same people." Undoubtedly Bacon would have given a similar answer to anyone attributing to him the plays of Shakespeare. Moreover, there is a wide difference between the art of writing dialogue for a novel and for a play. The novelist has in-numerable means of escape from difficulties which beset the dramatist. The skill required for success-fully conducting the story of a play by means limited to the use of dialogue makes the dramatist's art one of the most difficult to succeed in, and puts it outside the reach of all but the few and the specially gifted. To illustrate Shakespeare's constructive art it is only necessary to look at the old play of " King John," on which his own play is based. Then, to take an instance from a later play—" Twelfth Night "— Viola, when first seen on the stage, is a castaway, rescued by sailors. After an interval of one short scene she reappears as Cesario, the Duke's favourite page. How can the gap be most naturally bridged over ? Many dramatists would add dialogue de-tached from the story, but Shakespeare gives the necessary information in three words, which flash a picture upon the spectator's mind. Valentine says to Viola as they both enter the stage together : " If the Duke *continue these favours* towards you, Cesario, you are like to be much advanced," etc. In scheming

the sequence of incidents, and in suppressing ex-
planatory narrative, lies the art of the dramatist.
This result is not obtained without a good deal of
practice. Even Shakespeare could not have written
a play so compact as "Twelfth Night" at a period
when he was writing "The Two Gentlemen of
Verona."

In his young days Shakespeare must certainly
have read "Gorboduc," with its five acts, its five
dumb shows, and its chorus; he may, perhaps, have
seen it revived at Greenwich Palace, or elsewhere,
and have seen other plays of the kind which were
written in five acts by academicians—amateurs who
were anxious to air their learning before Queen Bess
at the Universities or at the Inns of Court. Then
there was Ben Jonson at hand to instruct his elder
rival on the superiority of Latin comedy. Chapman,
too, who was highly esteemed by clergy and scholars,
was within call to point out to "artless Will" the
merits of Senecan tragedy. In fact, the Bard of
Avon had good reason to know why his playhouse
dramas were despised by the learned, who, however,
were not justified in presuming that he was ignorant
of classical conventions simply because he chose to
ignore them.

No doubt it was possible in Shakespeare's time to
write plays in five acts for the public stage. We
know that at the Rose and Fortune theatres the
action of the play was often suspended to allow of
dancing and singing, though whether these intervals
for interludes came after the termination of each act
it is difficult to decide.

But if the four choruses in "Henry V." were
intended by Shakespeare to denote act divisions,

they are not so marked in the first folio; while
" The Tempest," which may have been divided into
acts by Shakespeare, has stage-directions which
suggest that it was not written originally for representation in the public theatre, but for the Court.

It must also be remembered that of the plays
wholly written by Shakespeare, with the one
exception of " The Tempest," all are so constructed
that characters who leave the stage at the end of an
episode are never the first to reappear, a reappear-
ance which would involve a short pause and an
empty stage; nor, even, does a character who ends
one of the acts marked in the folio ever begin the
one that follows, as Ben Jonson directs shall be done
in his tragedy of " Sejanus " (1616).   Can we reason-
ably suppose, then, that a method so consistently
carried out by Shakespeare throughout all his plays
respecting the exit and the re-entrance of characters
was due to mere accident, and not to deliberate
intention on the part of the dramatist ?   And in acted
drama the exact position where a pause comes in
the movement of the story is a matter of importance
to the proper understanding of the play.   Yet, in
the first collected edition of Shakespeare's plays
the divisions made are so irrelevant to the story
that Heminge and Condell may have considered
them as merely ornamental.   It may never have
occurred to them that the divisions would some
day be used as an authority for actors as well as for
readers.   The result has been disastrous to both.
A slavish adherence by the actor to these unfortunate
divisions for over two hundred years, has caused
the representation of Shakespeare's plays on the
stage to be in most cases unintelligent, if not almost

unintelligible; while, on the other hand, it has for an equally long period been the means of misleading scholars as to Shakespeare's method of dramatic construction. Until editors ignore the acts and scenes in the folio edition of 1623 and take the form of the play as it appears in the quartos—that is, without divisions—no progress can be made with the study of Shakespeare's dramatic art. It is now more generally recognized, especially by American scholars, that the folio divisions are a real stumbling-block and must go overboard. In some of the early comedies, perhaps, pauses can be made where the acts are marked, in the folio, without serious injury to the representation, but the comedies were written to be acted without break, and gain immensely when so given. Besides, the lengths of the present divisions are absurdly unequal. The last act of "Love's Labour's Lost" is more than twice the length of the first act, and nearly four times the length of the second and third acts. In a theatre, it should be the shortest act. Then, the "Comedy of Errors" was acted as an after-supper interlude at Gray's Inn. Time there would not allow of its having four intervals. Throughout Shakespeare's early and middle periods his plays in their dramatic form of construction provide no opportunity for regular intervals, nor should they ever have been divided into five acts. To put more than one break into "Romeo and Juliet," "The Merchant of Venice," "Macbeth," "King Lear," "Hamlet" (acting version) injures the drama. Shakespeare rarely cares to draw breath until he has reached the crisis, nor should the reader be expected to do so. And to halt for talk and refreshments on the eve of a crisis is to play havoc with the story. The crisis comes in the " Merchant of Venice" at that part of the play marked in the folio, Act III. Scene 1. But it is almost impossible for an actor to be animated in a scene following an *entr'acte*. The story of Macready and the ladder is a well known instance. The pause, if any, should come after the scene and not before it.

It cannot be urged too often that Shakespeare invented his dramatic construction to suit his own particular stage. And but for the special conditions of his playhouse, Shakespearian drama could never have come into being ; for Shakespeare's genius was not adapted to writing plays with intervals for music, as was done at Court. Unity of design was his aim. "Scene individable" is his motto. The internal evidence of the plays themselves proves this.

Dr. Johnson, then, was right to contend that Shakespeare wrote his plays as they were first printed "in one unbroken continuity," but to infer that "they ought now to be exhibited with short pauses interposed as often as the scene is changed, or any considerable time is required to pass," shows that he failed to grasp the real object for which Shakespeare adopted the continuous movement. An Elizabethan audience was absorbed by the story of the play, and thought little about lapse of time or change of place. There was only one locality recognized, and that one was the platform, which projected to the centre of the auditorium, where the story was recited. There was, besides, only one period, and that was "now," meaning the moment at which the events were being talked about or acted. All inconsistencies, then, that are apparent in the text, arising from change of place or break in the time, should be ignored in representing the play. It is no advantage to rearrange the order of the scenes, or to lower the curtain, or to make a pause in the progress of the story in order to call attention to change of place or interval of time. Whatever information Shakespeare wished the audience to have on these matters, he put into the mouths of his characters, and he expected the audience to accept it without any questioning or further illustration by actual presentation. Elizabethan folk-songs are sung without pausing between the verses; in this way attention is fixed on the story, and Shakespeare obtains the same result by dispensing with the empty stage.

Capell long ago pointed out the real difficulty, when he wrote in his preface: "Neither can the representation be managed nor the order and thread of the fable be properly conceived by the reader till the question of acts and scenes be adjusted." Unfortunately, Capell could prescribe no remedy. To this day these irregular divisions continue, and all our modern editions need reprinting and re-editing. One of the debts we owe to Shakespeare is to present his plays in their authentic form. This is due to him for what he was and for what he has done for us, as our greatest national poet and dramatist.

Some Mistakes of the Actors.

In Shakespeare's time the relations existing between the author and his actors were often strained. Those who interpreted the characters were blamed for more faults than their own, while the author, who was out of sight, had his reputation depending upon the skill of his interpreters. The actors, besides, were the author's paymasters, and often gave less for a new play than they paid for a silk doublet, while at the same time they were the absolute owners of all the dramas they produced. It was natural, then, for authors to taunt the actors with being men who thrived by speaking words which "better wits had framed."

The hired player, however, fared no better than the authors, and it was only those actors who had the right to pool the theatre takings who became rich. Before Shakespeare was forty years of age, he was earning a competent income out of his shares in two playhouses. No other dramatist of his time occupied so fortunate a position, nor probably one more isolated. As a tradesman's son, brought up at a grammar school only, he would have no standing among scholars, and as a writer of plays he was the "upstart crow," taking the bread out of the mouths of those who had paid for a college education. Then the historical dramas which brought the Globe fame and fortune were not calculated to please at Court, because neither the Queen nor the nobility cared to see their ancestors walking the public stages, unmasked, showing authority robbed of its sincerity and of its sanctity. Across the Thames stood the Blackfriars, where the children of the Chapel Royal, backed by royal favour, were rapidly becoming the attraction among the leaders of fashion and culture. These patrons upheld a class of entertainment with which Shakespeare had no sympathy. So the master spirit of the Elizabethan drama, like Beethoven, withdrew from the crowd to work out his own destiny, and to perfect himself in an art that fascinated him, and for which his practical life in the theatre, and his independence, gave him exceptional opportunity for experiment. During his last ten years in London he wrote some dozen or more plays, all of them of supreme merit. That they were dramas far in advance of the requirements of the day is probable, since few of them were printed during the poet's lifetime. Some of them, perhaps, were acted "not above once." He had outgrown, indeed, the theatrical taste of the day, and now only cared for plays which were "well digested in the scenes," meaning well constructed. But this was an achievement which no dramatist of his time attempted, unless it was Ben Jonson, who wrote artificial comedy after the classical models. Shakespeare, however, wanted the art of the theatre to imitate Nature, and he contrived to make speech and story appear natural; and, indeed, his contemporaries mistook this art for Nature, and thought it the work of an untutored mind and an unskilled hand. Even to-day many actors are under the impression that Shakespeare would have sanctioned as improvements the liberties now taken on the stage with his plays. Perhaps, also, his own fellow-actors failed to interpret his dramas entirely in accordance with his wishes; and yet his art is so vital and so vividly impressed on the printed page of the "authentic copies" that there is little justification for misrepresenting it. There is an anecdote about Mrs. Siddons, to the effect that when again reading over the part of Lady Macbeth, after her retirement from the stage, she was amazed to find some new points in the character "which had never struck her before"!   A confession which would seem incredible were it not known how apt English actors are to base the study of their parts not on the text, but on stage traditions, which often are valueless, because unauthorized.   Yet no actor should defend a conception of character which is shown to be at variance with the author's words.

The only copies of Shakespeare's plays which can with any authority be called acting-versions are the quartos, published during the poet's lifetime, and these are not acting-versions in the modern sense of the term, because, with the exception of textual errors, or abbreviations of dialogue, there is no shortening of the play by the omission of entire scenes or characters.   The early quartos, with the notable exceptions of the 1599 "Romeo and Juliet," the 1604 "Hamlet," and the 1609 "Troilus and Cressida," have the appearance of being made up from actors' parts, or taken down by shorthand writers during performances.   In consequence, they are less esteemed by the literary expert than are the plays as they appear printed in the first folio ; yet to the actors they provide information which cannot be found elsewhere.   That in some of these quartos the text is corrupt may be explained by the difficulty of taking down dialogue spoken rapidly from the stage, but at the same time it is unlikely that the note-takers went out of their way to describe any movement which they did not actually see carried out by the actors.   From the title-page of " The Merchant of Venice " it is evident that the copyist saw the play acted differently from the way it is now acted.   Take, for instance, the headline which is worded : " The comicall Historie of the

Merchant of Venice "; and the title-page, which sets
forth the " extreme crueltie of Shylocke the Jewe
towards the sayd Merchant, in cutting a just pound
of his flesh, and the obtayning of Portia by the
choyse of three chests." These two stories, which
are continued in alternate scenes throughout most
of the play, were to the Elizabethans regarded as
of equal importance. To-day the title-page would
have to be rewritten, and might run thus : " The
tragicall Historie of the Jewe of Venice, with the
extreme injustice of Portia towards the sayd Jewe
in denying him the right to cut a just pound of the
Merchant's flesh, together with the obtayning of the
rich heiress by the prodigal Bassanio." Over the
Shylock controversy enough ink has been wasted
without adding more, but the shortening of all the
Portia scenes, and the omission of the Prince of
Aragon, one of the three suitors, and one who
provides excellent comedy, are indefensible mutilations.

The title-page of the 1600 quarto of " Henry V."
mentions Henry's " battell fought at Agin Court, in
France, togither with Auntient Pistoll." " Swagger-
ing Pistoll," like Falstaff, had become a delight to
the town. The play is, in fact, not a " chronicle
history," but a slice out of history, and not of well-
made history either, since the evils of Henry's un-
just wars are not touched upon. Then Shakespeare's
King is an endless talker, while in reality he was
the most silent of men. It was ostensibly a " Jingo "
play, written to open the Globe playhouse with a
patriotic flourish of trumpets. Its object, besides,
was to please those Londoners who had not forgotten 1588, when Englishmen faced a similar ordeal

to that at Agincourt, and came out victorious, not because they had the means but the men. The interest of this drama, to the Elizabethan playgoer, depended on the knowledge that a handful of starved and ragged soldiers had won a decisive battle over an army which was its superior in numbers and equipment, and contained all the pride and chivalry of the French nation. And the stage-direction in the folio indicates the contrast thus : " *Enter the King and his poore Souldiers.*" On the modern stage, however, this direction is ignored, though perhaps it has never been noticed. The whole evening is taken up by the evolutions of a handsome young prince, gorgeously dressed, and spotlessly clean, newly come from his military tailor, together with a large number of equally well-dressed and well-fed soldiers, who tramp after him on and off the stage, not a penny the worse for all the hardships they are supposed to have encountered! Of the French episodes two are omitted and the rest mutilated, while no prominence is given to them, nor is the numerical superiority of the French indicated. Nothing is seen of its army beyond the leaders and their one or two attendants, who are thrust into the contracted space of a front scene. This seems rather an upside down way to act the play!

Among the early quartos, the two most interesting to the actor are the first and second editions of " Romeo and Juliet," because they show how Shakespeare adapted his art to the stage of his time. From them it may be inferred that characters on the stage did not always retire from view when they had finished speaking their lines. This, perhaps, was a necessity due to the presence of spectators on the platform, who made, as it were, an outer ring round the forefront or acting part of the stage. Romeo therefore did not leave the stage in the balcony episode, where Juliet is made to call him back again. He merely retired to the side of the platform, among the gallants. When Romeo hears of his banishment, the direction to the Nurse is "*Enter and Knocke*," which means that she comes in at the door of the tiring-house and remains at one side of the stage, probably knocking the floor with her crutch. After three knocks there is again the direction "*Enter*," when, on hearing her cue, she moves from the side into the centre of the stage to join in the dialogue. In this same quarto she and not the Friar is directed to snatch the dagger from Romeo, an evidence that this so-called "traditional-business," still in use, is not of Shakespeare's time. Another stage-direction shows how characters denoted change of locality merely by walking round the inner stage. No doubt this "business" was done to keep the spectators on the stage from chattering, which might easily happen whenever the actors left the forefront of the platform.

With regard to the first quarto of "Hamlet," and its probable history, something will be said later on. But it might be well here to call attention to the three stage-directions in this quarto, which have dropped out of all the subsequent editions, and which elucidate the context. Ophelia, in her "mad" scene, did not bring in flowers, but had a lute in her hands. There would be no need for the Queen so minutely to describe Ophelia's flowers at the time of her death if she had been previously seen with the garlands. The ghost, when in the Queen's chamber, wore a dressing-gown, not armour, probably the same gown he wore at the time of his death; Hamlet is overwhelmed with horror at this pitiful sight of his father. And Ophelia's body was followed to the grave by villagers and a solitary priest, who took no further part in the ceremony.

Elizabethan players had an advantage over modern actors in that they could more readily appreciate the construction of Shakespeare's plays. They knew that the dramatist's characters mutually supported each other within a definite dramatic structure, and that it was the business of the actor to preserve the author's framework. This attitude towards the play grew naturally out of the conditions belonging to their theatre, for unless the plot were adhered to, confusion would have arisen in the matter of entrances and exits, causing the continuity of the movement to be interrupted.

After the Restoration, when the public theatres were reopened, the "fable" ceased to have the same importance attached to it by the actors, and attention became more and more centred on those characters which were good acting parts. In 1773 appeared a collected edition of Shakespeare's plays, "As they are now performed at the Theatres Royal, Regulated from the Prompt Books of each House." The volumes were dedicated to Garrick, whom Bell, the compiler, pronounced to be "the best illustrator of, and the best living comment on, Shakespeare that ever has appeared or possibly ever will grace the British stage"; a statement which is qualified by the remark of Capell that "Garrick spoke many speeches of Shakespeare as if he did not understand them." Garrick, however, expresses his fear lest—

"the prunings, transpositions, or other alterations which in his province as a manager he had often found necessary to make or adopt with regard to the text, for the convenience of representation or accommodation to the powers and capacities of his performers, might be misconstrued into a critical presumption of offering to the *literati* a reformed and more correct edition of our author's works ; this being by no means his intention."

The reader need only examine one of the plays in Bell's "Companion to the Theatre" to understand Garrick's modesty as to his "prunings." Take the actor's stage-version of "Macbeth"—one of Bell's notes states, "This play, even amidst the fine sentiments it contains, would shrink before criticism did not Macbeth and his lady afford such uncommon scope for acting merit. Upon the whole, it is a fine drama with some gross blemishes." Apparently the "blemishes" are only found in those scenes where Macbeth or his wife do not appear, for Bell continues :

"The part of the porter is properly omitted. . . ."

"The flat, uninteresting scene, between Lenox and another useless Lord, is properly omitted. . . ."

"Here Shakespeare, as if the vigorous exertion of his faculties in the preceding scene required relaxation, has given us a most trifling, superfluous dialogue between Lady Macduff, Rosse, and her son, merely that another murder may be committed on the stage. We heartily concur in and approve of striking out the greater part of it. . . ."

"There are about eighty lines of this scene (Macduff's) omitted, which, retained, would render it painfully tedious, and, indeed, we think them as little deserving of the closet as of the stage," etc.

It does not seem to have struck Garrick that the scenes he "pruned" might have some significance in the scheme of the author's drama independently of their individual characteristics.

To take another instance. In Garrick's version of "Romeo and Juliet," reprinted in Dolby's "British Theatre" (1823), the following paragraph is inserted underneath the list of characters :

"The scenery in 'Romeo and Juliet' at Covent Garden this season (1823) is very grand. That of the 'Funeral of Juliet' is truly solemn and impressive. The architectural arrangement of the interior of the church is most chaste and appropriate : the slow approach of the funeral procession, the tolling of the bell, and the heart-saddening tones of the choristers, swelling in all the sublime richness of the minor key, make an impression on the feelings of the auditory which can never be forgotten."

Here, then, are illustrations, in two plays, of methods adopted by actors—methods still in use— which are a direct interference with the poet's dramatic intentions. They are methods, moreover, which Elizabethan actors would have regarded as unintelligent, because they turned good drama into bad drama, and created inconsistencies between character and situation. The earliest acting-version of "Romeo and Juliet" (1597) has some eight hundred lines less than the unshortened play (1599), and yet there is no entire scene omitted, nor any of the characters; and those scenes which have dropped out of the play, on the modern stage, are those least curtailed in the 1597 version. In the first acting-version of "Hamlet," published in 1603, there is still more striking evidence of the Elizabethan actor's skill in compressing a play of Shakespeare's when it was necessary. Not only was the play considerably shortened, without the omission of scenes and characters, but it was slightly reconstructed. Herr Emile Devrient, the greatest exponent of the part of Hamlet in Germany, contended that this first quarto was a better constructed play than either the 1604 version or that of the folio. In fact, with the faulty dialogue amended from the perfect text, this 1603 actor's copy, which has 1,757 fewer lines than in the full play, and 557 lines less than in the modern acting edition, would be the best model from which to shorten the play so as to bring it within the limit of a two hours' representation. That Shakespeare sanctioned either the compression or the reconstruction for use in the Globe is not likely. But that he tolerated the alterations is possible, since he would recognize that his own less regular plot, though more artistically suited as the framework for Hamlet's irregular mind, was too subtle and elaborate to be effective on the public stage.

With regard to acting-versions, therefore, it may be contended that the interests of the author are more often than not opposed to those of the modern actor in so far as the latter considers the author's drama to be tedious whenever it fails to enhance the acting merits of some particular character or characters in the play. Thus it is questionable whether, in the absence of the author, the actors are the persons best qualified to make stage-versions of his dramas. Their point of view is rarely the same as that of the author, and if it is necessary to shorten a play they can hardly be expected to undertake the work entirely to the satisfaction of the author, nor yet in the interests of the public, since

the value of the fable may or may not be a matter
of moment to an actor. If, then, Shakespeare's plays
are a valuable asset to the artistic wealth of the
nation, the amount of "pruning" they require for
the stage should be determined by competent experts. Unfortunately, actors believe that a scholar
is not qualified to advise on the matter, owing to
his lack of what they call "a sense of the theatre."
This "sense" would no doubt be differently interpreted by different actors. Broadly speaking, it
may be taken to mean the ability to forecast what
degree of emotion or sympathy certain incidents can
arouse in an audience when they are seen represented on the stage. Pope rejected the Gonzalo
dialogue in the second act of "The Tempest,"
asserting that it was not Shakespeare's because
courtiers who had been just shipwrecked on a desert
island would not indulge in idle gossip! Here
Pope missed the theatre point of view. The audience
see in the first act an old man who once had been a
King, but who was cruelly and unjustly thrust out of
his kingdom, and exposed with his baby daughter in
a frail and rotten bark to the mercy of the perilous
ocean. Moreover, it hears that the very men who
did this wrong are now themselves shipwrecked on
this enchanted island, where Prospero is living.
What the audience is curious to see, then, in the
second act, is not noblemen who are suffering from
shipwreck, but ignoble men, who merit the contempt
of those who look upon them, and who deserve the
just rebuke they receive from the man who is once
more restored to his rights. The question as to
what these noblemen have themselves suffered in
the course of being shipwrecked, Shakespeare

rightly judged was not one that an audience, under the circumstances, could be interested in. Then, again, to take a textual illustration from "King Lear" quoted by Steevens, the commentator. He writes in his "Advertisement to the Reader":

"The dialogue might, indeed, sometimes be lengthened by yet other insertions than have been made (from the quartos), without advantage either to its spirit or beauty, as in the following instance:

> "'LEAR. No.
> "'KENT. Yes.
> "'LEAR. No, I say.
> "'KENT. I say, yea.'

"Here the quartos add:

> "'LEAR. *No, no ; they would not*
> "'KENT. *Yes ; they have.*'

"By the admission of the negation and affirmation, would any new idea be gained?"

The answer given by the actor is, "Certainly! The added words from the quartos give the idea of reality and character." It is inconceivable that Shakespeare, himself an actor, omitted the additional lines. Without this reiteration, the expression of Lear's amazement at the indignity put upon his servant cannot be adequately tuned by the actor, nor yet be consistent with his character. This, then, is the dilemma with regard to stage-versions; scholars are hampered in their judgment by want of knowledge of the art of the theatre; and actors by their bias for good acting parts, or, in other words, for parts which are always in view of the audience.

As to elocution, it may be well to recall what an Antwerp merchant who had for many years resided in London said of the English people, about the year 1588. He then observed that "they do not speak from the chest like the Germans, but prattle only with the tongue." The word "prattle" is used in the same sense by Shakespeare in his play of "Richard the Second."* In the "Stage Player's Complaint," we find an actor making use of the expression, "Oh, the times when my tongue hath ranne as fast upon the Sceane as a Windebanke's pen over the ocean." Added to this, there is the celebrated speech to the players, in which Hamlet directs the actors to speak "trippingly on the tongue." There can be no doubt, therefore, that Shakespeare's verse was spoken on the stage of the Globe easily and rapidly. And the actor had the advantage of standing well within the building in a position now occupied by the stalls, nor were audiences then stowed away under deep projecting galleries. But unless English actors can recover the art of speaking Shakespeare's verse, his plays will never again enjoy the favour they once had. Poetry may require a greater elevation of style in its elocution than prose, but in either case the fundamental condition is that of representing life, and as George Lewes ably puts it, "all obvious violations of the truths of life are errors in art." In the delivery of verse, therefore, on the stage, the audience should never be made to feel that the tones are unusual. They should still follow the laws of speaking, and not those of singing. But our actors, who excel in modern plays by the truth and force of their presentation of life, when they appear in Shakespeare make use of an elocution that no human being

* See quotation on p. 21.

was ever known to indulge in. They employ, besides, a redundancy of emphasis which destroys all meaning of the words and all resemblance to natural speech. It is necessary to bear in mind that, when dramatic dialogue is written in verse, there are more words put into a sentence than are needed to convey the actual thought that is uppermost in the speaker's mind; in order, therefore, to give his delivery an appearance of spontaneity, the actor should arrest the attention of the listener by the accentuation of those words which convey the central idea or thought of the speech he is uttering, and should keep in the background, by means of modulation and deflection of voice, the words with which that thought is ornamented. Macbeth should say:

> "That but this BLOW
> Might be the be-all and the end-all HERE,
> But HERE, upon this bank and shoal of time,
> We'd jump the life to COME.—But in these cases
> We still have judgment HERE; that we but teach
> BLOODY instructions, which, being taught, RETURN
> To plague the INVENTOR."

If the emphasis fall upon the words marked, then these and no others should be the words inflected; but modern actors, if they inflect the right words, inflect the wrong ones too, until it becomes impossible for the listener to identify the sense by the sound. This artificial way of speaking verse seems traditional to the eighteenth century. David Garrick and Edmund Kean no doubt used a more natural delivery, and also Mrs. Siddons, though some of her exaggerations of emphasis probably were never heard at the Globe. Shakespeare would hardly have endorsed her reading of Lady Macbeth's

words, "Give ME the daggers!" There was nobody
else to whom Macbeth could give them. At moments
of tension, speech is always direct. A lady, *tête à tête*
with her husband at the breakfast-table, enjoying an
altercation over the contents of the newspaper,
would surely indicate the natural emphasis by ex-
claiming, "GIVE me the newspaper!" words that
can, in this way, be spoken in half the time that
Mrs. Siddons took to speak hers. The two and a
half hours in which a play in Shakespeare's time
was often acted would not be possible to-day, even
without delays for acts and scenes, with the methods
of elocution now in vogue. It is legitimate for
Romeo to exclaim in his farewell to Juliet:

> " EYES, look your last !
> ARMS, take your last embrace !"

or he may say:

> " Eyes, look your LAST !
> Arms, take your last EMBRACE !"

but it is not correct to say:

> " EYES, look your LAST !
> ARMS, take your last EMBRACE !"

which every Romeo persists in saying to-day; and
this method of duplicating emphasis, being used by
all the actors throughout the whole play, the time
taken up in speaking it is at once doubled. Hence
the need for excessive " prunings."

To sum up the arguments: Shakespeare's dramatic
art, which is unique of its kind, cannot to-day be
properly understood or appreciated on the stage for
the following reasons: (1) Because editors print the

plays as if they were five-act dramas, which they are not; (2) because actors, in their stage versions, mutilate the "fable," and interpolate pictorial effects where none are intended ; (3) because, also, actors use a faulty and artificial elocution, unsuited to the poet's verse. These causes, combined, oust Shakespeare's original plays from the theatre, and impose in their place pseudo-classical dramas which are not of his making, nor of his time. To remedy this evil it is necessary to insist that the early quartos alone represent Shakespeare's form of construction and his method of representation, and that for the purpose of determining the text these same quartos should be collated with the first folio, with occasional reference to modern editions. Cheap facsimiles of the quartos as well as the folio should be accessible to actors, and from these an attempt should be made to standardize stage-versions of Shakespeare's most popular plays, and these stage-versions should be the joint work of scholars and actors.

Perhaps what is important for the general public to recognize is that the acting-versions of Shakespeare's plays, the interpretation given to his characters, and the actor's " readings " have altered but little during the last two hundred years, so that the performances given on the stage to-day are chiefly founded upon traditions which never came into touch with Elizabethan times. More and more, therefore, must it be realized that if an actor wishes to interpret the plays intelligently, he must shut his eyes to all that has taken place on the stage since the poet's time, turning to Shakespeare's text and trusting to that alone for inspiration.

The Character of Lady Macbeth.

I should never think, for instance, of contesting an actress's right to represent Lady Macbeth as a charming, insinuating woman, if she really sees the figure that way. I may be surprised at such a vision ; but so far from being scandalized, I am positively thankful for the extension of knowledge, of pleasure, that she is able to open to me.— HENRY JAMES.

The introduction of women players led to one of the evils connected with the star system. So long as boys acted the women's parts there was no danger of any woman's character being made over-prominent to the extent of unbalancing the play. But when Mrs. Siddons became famous by her impersonation of Lady Macbeth, it may be contended, without prejudice to the talent of the actress, that the character ceased to represent Shakespeare's point of view. This is the more to be regretted in view of Mrs. Siddons' confession that her personality was not suited to the part. There was, besides, another drawback unfortunately in that, during the eighteenth century, the part of Lady Macduff dropped out of the playbill, thus removing from the play the one person in it whose presence was necessary for the proper understanding of Lady Macbeth's character. The appearance of Lady Macduff on the stage affords opportunity for the reflection that Duncan's murder would never have taken place had she been Macbeth's wife. Yet she, too, has shortcomings to which she falls a victim, for when the assassins are at her door she exclaims :

> "Whither should I fly ?
> I have done no harm. But I remember now
> I am in this earthly world, where to do harm
> Is often laudable ; to do good, sometime,

> Accounted dangerous folly: why then, alas !
> Do I put up that womanly defence,
> To say, I have done no harm ?"

Now, admirable as this reflection is from an ethical standpoint, it is not appropriate to the moment, and in Lady Macbeth's eyes it would have been "dangerous folly" to talk moral platitudes at such a time.   In fact, if the mistress of Inverness Castle had been placed in Lady Macduff's cruel position, it is more than likely she would have had the courage and the energy to save her own life and those of her children from the fury of Macbeth.   Nor is it inconceivable that if Lady Macbeth had married a man of stronger moral fibre than her husband, she might have lived a useful life, loved and respected by all who knew her.   And yet, unhappily for both women, neither Macbeth nor Macduff were fine types of manhood.

Another idea which needs to be cleared out of the way is that of the unusual enormity of Lady Macbeth's crime in contriving the death of a man who was her guest.   Shakespeare's audience knew that a sovereign was never immune from assassination. Queen Elizabeth's life became the mark for assassin after assassin.   Moreover, the Catholics contended that "good Queen Bess," by beheading Mary Stuart, had murdered a woman who was her guest and who had come into her kingdom assured of protection. There was something childish about Duncan's credulity in face of the treachery he had already experienced from the first Thane of Cawdor.   In a monarch whose position was open to attack from the jealousy of his nobles, Duncan's conduct showed an almost incredible want of caution.   In fact, it was his unguarded confidence which brought about his death. No onlooker in the Globe playhouse ever thought the murder of this King at Inverness to be an improbable or unusual occurrence. And this inference suggests another of even more importance, namely, the period in which Shakespeare's tragedy is placed. When the poet-dramatist demanded that his actors should hold the mirror up to Nature, it was not the nature of the Greeks, nor of the Romans, nor of the early Britons that he meant. The spirit of the Italian Renaissance, with its humanism and intellectuality, had taken too strong a hold upon the imagination of Englishmen to allow of their playgoers being interested in the puppets of a bygone age. Shakespeare had no need to look beyond his own time to find his Lady Macbeth. There were many women still existing who were uninfluenced by the didactic teaching of the Puritans and their love of moral introspection. Queen Elizabeth herself was an instance. As the historian Green points out, we track her through her tortuous maze of lying and intrigue until we find that she revelled in byways and crooked ways, and yet was adored by her subjects for a womanliness she, in reality, never possessed. And this love of shuffling and lack of all genuine religious emotion failed utterly to blur the brightness of the national ideal. Or, to take her rival, Mary Stuart. The rough Scottish nobles owned that there was in her some enchantment whereby men were bewitched. "Her beauty," writes Green, "her exquisite grace of manner, her generosity of temper and warmth of affection, her frankness of speech, her sensibility, her gaiety, her womanly tears, her manlike courage, the play and freedom of her nature . . . flung a spell over friend or foe which has only deepened with the lapse of years." And yet this piece of feminine fascination visited her sick husband, Darnley, in his lonely house near Holyrood Palace, in which he was lodged by her order, kissed him, bade him farewell, and rode gaily back to a dance within two hours of the terrible explosion which deprived him of his life, a murder that was attributed to Bothwell, and at which Mary herself may easily have connived.

And so it was with Lady Macbeth. Murder, to those who were not injured by it, was no crime in her opinion, and excited neither terror nor remorse. She was to the last unconscious of being criminal or sinful. Her life was the playing of a red-handed game by one who thought herself innocent. For this reason she could walk placidly through any evil she contemplated. She knew that her persuasive power over men lay in her womanliness, and that in this there was nothing compromising. Unlike her husband, her face betrayed no moral conflict. The Puritan spirit had never penetrated her own nature. Whatever her outward religion might be, she was at heart a materialist, not from conviction, but from shallowness, due to the absence of all the higher powers of reflection and imagination. Banquo is dead, and therefore she knows that it is impossible for him to come out of his grave to torment his murderer. It is only necessary to wash the blood from her hands, and that will clear away the consequences. Even the " spirits," to which her husband has alluded ; those which she mockingly invokes to her feminine aid, have no reality to her, because they have no material whereabouts.

So that her husband's talk about conscience and retribution is unintelligible to her. She knows that what he would do "wrongly" he would like to do "holily," because she has heard about the Ten Commandments; but these things have no meaning for her, they do not come within her experience. With her limited outlook, the beginning and end of everything necessary for her husband's success in life is that he should be practical, inventive, and never appear embarrassed.

The most marked feature, then, in Lady Macbeth's character is her femininity, and Shakespeare dwells upon this trait throughout her career. In the first place, no one at Inverness Castle suspects that she is accessory to the terrible crime. Macduff is distressed at the mere thought of telling her what has happened. The woman who would have been trampled under foot in the courtyard on that eventful night, if the truth about her had been known, becomes the centre of immediate anxiety when she faints, or feigns to faint, to rescue her husband from a perilous position. Duncan could not find words to express his delight at her charm as a hostess. The guests at the royal coronation banquet grieve that she should be exposed to a trying ordeal through her husband's extraordinary behaviour. The doctor who overhears her dying confessions is "mated" and "amazed" and incredulous at the thought of her self-implications. One voice speaks of her with harshness, and it is that of the son of the murdered King, and then only at the close of the play. If, again, we turn to her own reflections, it is always her woman's weakness which she dreads may defeat her purpose. Murder is something foreign to her

5

temperament; the details are ugly and revolting; the sight of blood may unnerve her. She can do the crime herself if she can accomplish it without seeing the wound the dagger will make; but she evidently imagines that her husband, who has killed men in battle, can do it better, and this conviction becomes a moral certainty when she is confronted with the pathetic figure of that trusting, white face, with its whiter hair, so like her own father's. When the fatal moment arrives she cannot meet her husband in her normal mood, but has recourse to the wine-cup, not because she shrinks from the notion of murder, but from dislike for the details of the operation. She has, besides, all the little partialities of a woman who delights in the beauty of the innocent flower and in perfumes of Arabia. Then the thought of being a Queen and wearing a real crown is an intense delight to her. Macbeth knew of her weakness for finery when he sought her approval of the deed; it was his bribe for her help. And women of Lady Macbeth's temperament do not care to be disappointed of their pleasures. To break promise in these matters, she tells her husband, is as cruel as it would be for her to kill her own child, that being a crime of which she is incapable, for she is a devoted mother.

Nor must the marked contrast between her attitude before and after the crime be overlooked. At its inception, murder is a mere means to an end, which creates no misgivings in her mind. She sees "the future in the instant," a future which gives her "the golden round," and bestows on her husband "sovereign sway and masterdom." But no sooner is the crime committed than her optimism fails her, for her husband seems no nearer to "masterdom" than he was before. After the coronation there comes her tragic reflection that the murder was a mistake. Unfortunately for her, it was worse than a mistake; it was a blunder for which her husband deposes her authority. No longer does he listen to her counsels, and although she has not lost any of her charm or her womanliness, her spell over him has gone for ever. Never again can she say, "From this time such I account thy love," but merely ejaculates, "Did you send to him, *sir?*" No such cruel awakening was in store for her husband. He knew from the first that his crime must bring retribution and arouse the anger of the gods; but she, for her part, foresaw no harm and no consequences. It is the shock of her failure which paralyzes her power for further action. She is not repentant, because she is unconscious of having sinned, and to the last she is at a loss to understand why murdering an old man in his bed has divorced her husband's affection from her, and turned him into a bloodthirsty tyrant. Her brain is not big enough to take in what all these things mean, and under strain of anxiety and disappointment her mind gives way. This, then, is the Lady Macbeth that Mrs. Siddons identifies as "a character which, I believe, is generally allowed to be most captivating to the other sex, fair, feminine, nay, perhaps even fragile. Such a combination only, respectable in energy and strength of mind and captivating in feminine loveliness, could have composed a charm of such potency as to fascinate the mind of a hero so dauntless as Macbeth."

There is no portrait in Shakespeare's gallery of

women more generally misunderstood than this one, the reason, perhaps, being that the poet has not been credited with the desire or experience to draw a type of woman so obviously disingenuous. But no one can read Shakespeare aright who thinks that the men and women who live in our age do not resemble those who lived in his time. Not until we read the Lady Macduff scene carefully can we grasp the kind of woman Shakespeare had in his mind. Then it will be evident that the real criminal in the play is Macbeth, whose conscience warns him that "unnatural deeds beget unnatural troubles," and who, against his better judgment, allows himself to be influenced, out of connubial love, into an action of which he knows his wife to be incapable of foreseeing the consequences. When disaster follows, we can set up that "womanly defence" for her and say, "she meant no harm." There is no such appeal possible for her husband, who is condemned from the first out of his own mouth.

Shakespeare, it must be remembered, wrote the play of "Macbeth" probably about 1605, when the Globe actors were still competing with the children at Blackfriars, who, with their fine music, gorgeous costumes, and "candlelight," attracted the well-to-do people of the town. In this tragedy, therefore, Shakespeare revives interest in the Faustus legend, once so popular at a rival house. The notion that man could set himself up in opposition to the Deity was due to the teaching of the Reformation. If man could defy the supremacy of the Pope, might he not challenge also Omniscience Itself? Having once tasted of the Tree of Knowledge, Faustus will not rest until he can know all, can do all, and dare all :

> " Till swoln with cunning of a self-conceit,
> His waxen wings did mount above his reach,
> And, melting, heavens conspir'd his overthrow."

And Hecate prophesies of Macbeth that—

> " He shall spurn fate, scorn death, and bear
> His hopes 'bove wisdom, grace, and fear ;
> And you all know security
> Is mortals' chiefest enemy."

To playgoers at the Globe, then, the interest in the play of " Macbeth " lay in the man's daring attempt to defeat the supernatural. The scheme of drama requires that Macbeth, like Faustus, shall be the pivot of the play. Of necessity, then, it is an error of judgment for a stage-manager to allow the part of Lady Macbeth to be overacted. Apart from the witches, there are only two women in the play, neither of whom are of more than common mould. They are alike in this, that both are by nature domestic, and appreciate family ties ; while in other respects they are finely contrasted, and represent the old and the new type of character which must have so interested dramatists in Shakespeare's time—that of the Renaissance or Italian type, upholding the doctrine of expediency ; and that of the Reformation, demanding obedience to conscience.

Shakespeare's Jew and Marlowe's Christians.*

In the opinion of Heinrich Heine, Shylock, as a typical study of Judaism, was merely a caricature. If this is a correct estimate of the character, then

* *The Westminster Review*, January, 1909.

Shakespeare's Jew is the Elizabethan Christian's notion of an infidel in much the same way as the modern stage Paddy is the Englishman's idea of an Irishman. Shakespeare, in fact, thrusts the conventional usurer of the old Latin comedy into a play of love and chance and money-bags in order to serve the purpose of a stage villain, and calls him a Jew. Shylock is an isolated figure, unsociable, parsimonious, and relentless, who tries to inflict harm on those who envy him his wealth and hate him for his avarice.

Perhaps it is this marked isolation in which the dramatist has placed Shylock that tempts the modern actor to represent him as a victim of religious persecution, and therefore as one who does not merit the misfortune that falls upon him. In this way the figure becomes tragic, and, contrary to the dramatist's intention, is made the leading part; so that when the Jew finally leaves the stage, the interest of the audience goes with him. But if Shakespeare intended his comedy to produce this impression, he was at fault in writing a last act in which every character that appears is evidently not aware that Shylock's defeat was undeserved; nor is there any evidence to show that Shakespeare designed his comedy as a satire on the inhumanity of Christians. How then has it been brought about that, while the exigencies of the drama require Shylock to be the wrongdoer, he now appears on the stage as the one who is wronged?

In the first place, a change of opinion in a nation's religion or politics causes a change in the theatre. New plays are written to give expression to the new sentiment, and the old plays, when revived, must be modified or readjusted to bring them in touch with the new opinions. To meet this marked change in public taste managers and actors are forced to abandon convention. It is useless at such a time to quote authorities. Public opinion is arbitrary, and the genius of a Macklin or a Kean would fail to arouse interest if it were out of sympathy with the newly awakened conscience. A popular actor is tempted, therefore, to show the old figure in the light of the new sentiment, and his impersonation is then set up as a model to which every contemporary candidate for favour is expected to conform.

It must be conceded, also, that our playgoers are rarely familiar with the text of Shakespeare's plays, and thus increased opportunity is given to the actor to overrule the author. Yet this does not explain why an interpretation, quite unjustified by the text, should find favour with many dramatic critics. If a sound judgment and true taste are to prevail among playgoers, criticism should dissociate history from sentiment and discriminate between old conventions and modern innovations. Few critics, however, care to separate themselves from the opinions of their day; in fact, so far as Shakespeare's plays are concerned, newspaper criticism is often limited to the business of reporting. Otherwise it is difficult to explain the chorus of unanimous approval with which the Press, as well as the public, hailed the new Shylock in the picturesque and sympathetic rendering given at the Lyceum in the early eighties.

Even if it be admitted that the terms of opprobrium with which Shylock is accosted by all the Christians in Shakespeare's comedy are unneces-

sarily harsh, even if it be granted that to Gratiano,
Solanio, and Salarino he is the "dog Jew," meaning
a creature outside the pale of heaven, yet if we
read between the lines it is evident that religious
differences are not the chief grievance. Shylock
is a Jew, therefore a moneylender; a moneylender,
therefore rich; rich, yet a miser, and therefore of
little value to the community, which remains un-
benefited by his usurious loans. This, in the eyes
of the Christian merchants, is the real significance
of the word Jew. The Catholic Church, by for-
bidding Christians to take interest, had unintention-
ally given the Jews a monopoly of the money-market,
but with it that odium which attaches to the usurer.
This point of view can be specially illustrated by
Marlowe's Barabas, in "The Jew of Malta," the pre-
cursor of Shylock. Barabas makes no secret as to
the unpopularity of his profession:

> " I have been zealous in the Jewish faith,
> Hard-hearted to the poor, a covetous wretch,
> That would for lucre's sake have sold my soul.
> A hundred for a hundred I have ta'en ;
> And now for store of wealth may I compare
> With all the Jews in Malta."

His riches are blessings reserved exclusively for
his race:

> " And thus are we on every side enriched :
> These are the blessings promised to the Jews."
>
> *   *   *   *   *
>
> " Rather had I a Jew be hated thus,
> Than pitied in a Christian poverty :"
>
> *   *   *   *   *
>
> " Aye, wealthier far than any Christian."
>
> *   *   *   *   *
>
> " What more may Heaven do for earthly man
> Than thus to pour out plenty in their laps."

This, then, was the Christian notion of the Jew in Shakespeare's time, and while we have no reason for supposing that it was Shakespeare's also, there is enough evidence to show that for the purpose of his story the dramatist adopted the prevalent opinion that the Jew was a man who lived solely for his wealth.   In the face of this knowledge it is difficult to understand the opinion of some commentators that Shylock was intended as a protest against Marlowe's " mere monster."   The similarity between Shylock and Barabas has been pointed out by Dr. Ward. Both love money, both hoard their wealth, both starve their servants to save expense, both defend their religion as well as their usury, both love to despoil the Christians and taunt them with their lack of fairness.   Of course, every good critic admits that there are two sides to an argument.   Even Sir Walter Scott, when reviewing a book, confesses to his son-in-law that his criticism might have been very different were the mandate *déchirer*.   And those who want to defame Shylock's character will not find it a difficult thing to do.   The following illustration of the character is given after the manner of a schoolboy's paraphrase :

Shylock thinks it folly to lend money without interest.   Jacob was blessed for thriving, even if he prospered by cunning means, and to thrive by any means short of stealing is to deserve God's blessing. Shylock can make money as quickly as ewes and rams can breed.   He will show how generous he can be towards Christians by lending Antonio money without asking a farthing of interest, pro- vided Antonio consents, by way of a joke, to lose a pound of his flesh if he should fail to repay the money on a special day ; and this pound to be taken from any part of his body which Shylock may choose, meaning, no doubt, nearest to the heart, so as to ensure death. Yet Bassanio need have no anxiety about the safety of his friend's life, because human flesh is not a marketable commodity like mutton or beef.

Shylock has a servant who eats too much, and is so lazy that the Jew is glad to part with him to the impecunious Bassanio, in the hope that Launcelot will help to squander his new master's " borrowed purse." For a similar reason he will himself go to Bassanio's feast, although his religion forbids him to eat with Christians. His daughter is not to have any pleasure from the masque, but to shut herself up in the house so that no sound of Christian masquerading may reach her ears. His last words to her are in praise of thrift.

The Jew's first exclamation on hearing that Jessica cannot be found is that he has lost a diamond worth 2,000 ducats. He would like to see his daughter dead at his feet if only he can have again the jewels that are in her ears, and find the ducats in her coffin. It is heartrending to think how Jessica has been squandering his treasures, and of the additional loss to him in having to pay Tubal for trying to find the girl ; yet it is gratify-ing to hear of Antonio's misfortunes ; and since the merchant is likely to become bankrupt it will be well to fee an officer in readiness to arrest him the moment the time of the bond expires. If only Antonio can be got out of the way, Shylock will be able to make as much money as ever he likes. With this thought to console him he goes to the synagogue to say his prayers.

When Antonio is arrested, Shylock demands the utmost penalty of the law because of a " lodged hate and a certain loathing " he bears the bankrupt. No amount of money will tempt him to forgo his rights, and the letter of the law must be observed in every detail ; not even a surgeon must be allowed on the spot in the hope of saving this lend-you-money-for-nothing merchant's life. When Portia frustrates his purpose and he finds the law against him, he can still ask that the loan be repaid "thrice" (Portia and Bassanio thought "twice" a sufficiently tempting offer). And when Portia points out that, as an alien, who has deliberately plotted to take the life of a Christian, Shylock's own life is forfeited, as well as the whole of his wealth, he still demands the return of his principal.

Now if we go back to the Latin Comedies and consider the origin of the moneylender, we find a type of character similar to that of Shylock. Molière's Harpagon, who is modelled on the miser of Plautus, has a strong resemblance to Barabas and to Shylock, although Shylock is undoubtedly the most human. Reference has already been made to the likeness between Barabas and Shylock, and it needs but a few illustrations to show the resemblance between the English and French miser. Both are moneylenders, who when asked for a loan declare that it is necessary for them to borrow the sum required from a friend. Sheridan makes little Moses do the same. Harpagon exclaims to his servant: "Ah, wretch, you are eating up all my wealth," and Shylock says the same thing to Launcelot. Harpagon's, "It is out of Christian charity that he covets my money," is not unlike the reproach of Shylock, "He was wont to lend out money for a Christian courtesy!" And "justice, impudent rascal, will soon give me satisfaction!" is with Shylock "the Duke shall grant me justice!" While if we compare the words which Molière puts into the mouths of those who revile the miser, they suggest the taunts thrown at Shylock. "I tell you frankly that you are the laughing-stock of everybody, and that nothing delights people more than to make game of you "; has its equivalent in the speech " Why, all the boys in Venice follow him," etc. And "never does anyone mention you, but under the name of Jew and usurer," tallies with Launcelot's " My master is a very Jew."   Other instances might be quoted.

Of course it cannot be overlooked that Shakespeare has given Shylock one speech of undoubted power which silences all his opponents.   For while the Christians are unconscious of any wrongdoing on their side towards the Jew, Shylock complains loudly and bitterly of the indignities thrust upon him by the Christians, and in that often-quoted speech beginning " Hath not a Jew eyes " he complains with an insistence which certainly claims consideration. Now in so far as Shylock resents the want of toler-ance shown him by the Christians, he is in the right and Shakespeare is with him ; but when he tries to justify his method of retaliation and schemes to take Antonio's life, not simply in order to revenge the indignities thrust upon him, but also that he may put more money into his purse, Shylock is in the wrong and Shakespeare is against him.   For it is obvious that Shylock does not seek the lives of Gratiano, Solanio, or Salarino, the men who called him the " dog Jew," or the life of the man who ran away with his daughter, but of the merchant who lends out money gratis, who helps the unfortunate debtors, and who exercises generosity and charity. Whatever blame attaches to the Christians on the score of intolerance, Antonio is the least offender, except in so far as it touches Shylock's pocket. And when Shylock the usurer asserts that a Christian is no better than a Jew, he forgets that Christianity, in its original conception and purpose, forbade the individual to prey on his fellow-creatures; and this is the Christianity which Antonio practises.

Finally it is the intention of the comedy, as Shakespeare has designed it, to illustrate the consequence of a too rigid adherence to the letter of the law. The terms of the bond to which Shylock clings so tenaciously, and for which he demands unquestioning obedience, ultimately endanger his own life and with it the whole of his property. Shylock falls a victim to his own plot in the same way that Barabas tumbles into his own burning caldron; but the Christians spare the Jew's life and half his wealth is restored to him, and restored to him by Antonio "the bankrupt," who is still himself greatly in need of money. That Shylock must in return for this mercy deny his faith is not in the eyes of the Christian a punishment or even an act of malice, but a means of salvation.

The basis, then, of Shakespeare's comedy, it is contended, is a romantic story of love and adventure. It shows us a lovable and high-minded heroine, her adventurous and fervent lover, and his unselfish friend, together with their merry companions and sweethearts. And into this happy throng, for the purpose of having a villain, the dramatist thrusts the morose and malicious usurer, who is intended to be laughed at and defeated, not primarily because he is a Jew, but because he is a curmudgeon; thus the prodigal defeats the miser.

If we look more closely into the two plays of Marlowe and Shakespeare, and compare not only

Barabas with Shylock, but also Marlowe's Christians with those of Shakespeare, we find a dissimilarity in the portraiture of the Christians so marked that it is impossible to ignore the idea that Shakespeare, perhaps, wished to protest not against Marlowe's "inhuman Jew," but against his pagan Christians. The variance, in fact, is too striking to be accidental, as the following table will show:

THE FAMOUS TRAGEDY OF THE RICH JEW OF MALTA.	THE MOST EXCELLENT HISTORY OF THE MERCHANT OF VENICE.
The play is named after the Jew who owns the argosies.	The play is named after the Christian who owns the argosies.
The Christians take forcible possession of all the Jew's wealth.	The Christians ask a loan of the Jew on business terms.
The Jew upbraids the Christians for quoting Scripture to defend their roguery.	The Christian upbraids the Jew for quoting Scripture to defend his roguery.
The Christians break faith with the Turks, and also with the Jew.	A Christian Court upholds the Jew's claim to his bond.
The Jew's daughter Abigail rescues her father's money from the Christians.	Jessica gives away her father's money to the Christians.
The Jew's servant helps his master to cheat the Christians.	Launcelot leaves his master to join the Christians.
Two Christians try to cajole the Jew of his daughter, and die victims to his treachery.	Lorenzo elopes with Jessica, and finally inherits the Jew's wealth.
Abigail becomes a Christian and is poisoned by her father.	Jessica becomes a Christian and is happy ever after.
The Jew is the means of saving the Christians from the Turks.	Portia saves the Christian from the Jew.
The Christians are accessory to the Jew's death, which is an act of treachery on their part.	The Christians spare the Jew's life, which is an act of mercy on their part.

It might be objected that the interval of seven years between the production of the two plays renders it improbable that Shakespeare would have intentionally contrasted his play with Marlowe's. But the popularity of "The Jew of Malta" exceeded that of any other contemporary play. Although it was not printed till 1604, it was produced in 1588, and references to it in contemporary plays continue to be found until 1609. Owing, besides, to Alleyne's extraordinary success as Barabas, the play continued to be acted at intervals until 1594, between which date and 1598 Shakespeare had written his own comedy. The setting-off, too, of play against play was a common practice, especially among the early Elizabethan dramatists, and Greene did not hesitate to avail himself of the success of Marlowe's "Doctor Faustus" to write his "Friar Bacon and Friar Bungay."

Now in so far as "The Jew of Malta" makes fun of friars and nuns, it would be considered legitimate amusement by a Protestant audience. We have a similar record on the French stage of revolutionary times when as M. Fleury remarks: "All the convents in France were shown up at the theatres, and the surest mode of drawing money to the treasury was to raise a laugh at the expense of the Veil." But Marlowe goes further than this. He attacks Christianity wantonly and aggressively, not only by portraying Barabas's contempt for the Christians, but by making the Christians contemptible in themselves, and wanting in all those virtues which were upheld in the newly accessible Gospels. They are without honour and chivalry or any sense of justice or loyalty. They are false and treacherous to

Jew and Turk alike, and Barabas can well say of them :

> " For I can see no fruits in all their faith,
> But malice, falsehood, and excessive pride,
> Which methinks fits not their profession."

Further, the Christians take by force the Jew's money to pay the city's tribute to the Turks, which after all is not paid, the Christians keeping the money for themselves.   It is but the bare truth that Barabas states when he mutters :

> " Who, of mere charity and Christian truth,
> To bring me to religious purity,
> And as it were in catechising sort,
> To make me mindful of my mortal sins,
> Against my will, and whether I would or no,
> Seized all I had, and thrust me out o' doors."

And Marlowe also makes Barabas say, indignant at the Christians' hypocrisy :

> " Is theft the ground of your religion ?
> *   *   *   *   *
> What, bring you scripture to confirm your wrongs ?
> Preach me not out of my possessions."

Scepticism is rampant throughout " The Jew of Malta," and Marlowe flaunts his opinions before a theatre full of Christians.   Not that it is contended that Marlowe was himself an atheist, but in " The Jew of Malta" he seems, perhaps out of a spirit of retaliation for the wanton attacks made upon him, to be bent on exposing to ridicule the upholders of the orthodox faith.   In Marlowe's " Faustus" the good angel, the aged pilgrim, and the final repentance satisfy the religious conscience, but his later play has no such compensations.   The boast of Barabas that, "some Jews are wicked as *all* Christians are," passes unchallenged.

Now it is unlikely that any member of Elizabeth's Court, any Protestant nobleman who was responsible for upholding the reformed faith, much less that any Catholic, could have been present at the performance of this play without protesting against the poet's attitude towards Christianity. Nor is it probable that the Lord Chamberlain's servants would overlook Marlowe's taunts at the national religion spoken from the citizens' playhouse. So that the poet-player whose sonnets were being circulated in the houses of the nobility, whose patron was the Earl of Southampton, the friend of Essex, and who had begun to be talked about at Court, might with advantage to himself expose the other side of the picture, and defend the abused Christians.

It remained then for Shakespeare to show that Christians, if they hated the infidel, were not in themselves contemptible. In addition to her many fascinations of mind and person, Portia possesses in an eminent degree a sense of honour and a love of mercy. The obligations imposed upon her by her father are religiously observed. Even when her lover is choosing the caskets, and a glance would have put him out of his misery, her attitude towards him is uncompromising. Later on she upholds the Jew's plea for justice, while at the same time she urges the more divine attribute of mercy.

Where Shakespeare, however, differs from Marlowe most strikingly is in the character of the Merchant after whom the comedy is named. Barabas has boasted that—

> " he from whom my most advantage comes
> Shall be my friend.
> This is the life we Jews are used to lead."

6

Then he naïvely adds :

> "And reason, too, for Christians do the like."

Now the dearest object of affection in the world for Antonio is Bassanio, and it is the knowledge that his beloved friend has a rival for his love in Portia, which causes Antonio's sadness ; yet he not only gives up his companion ungrudgingly to the enjoyment of greater happiness, but provides him with the necessary means ; and for this purpose he signs a perilous bond with his bitterest foe. Of necessity he dislikes Shylock, whose debtors he has so often saved from ruin. With Jessica's flight he had nothing to do. He certainly never sanctioned it. Moreover, when misfortune comes upon him he has no desire to escape from the penalty of the bond, and when he himself is in poverty he saves from a similar calamity a man who hates him. In face of these facts it is difficult to understand why Heine should consider Antonio unworthy to tie Shylock's shoelaces !

Again, Bassanio is often called a fortune-hunter, but without justification. He knew that he enjoyed the esteem and affection of Portia while her father was yet alive. The "speechless messages" of her eyes invited his return to Belmont. On his arrival he finds that she can no longer dispose of herself, and yet, unlike most of the other suitors, he does not on that account withdraw : he wins her because he loves her and knows that love is worth more than gold or silver. When he hears of Antonio's danger he rushes to his friend's side to offer his own life to save him. It is to be noticed also that Portia's esteem for Antonio's openly proclaimed virtues is drawn from a comparison with those of Bassanio. They are by no means contemptible.

Jessica, again, who must be counted among the Christians, finds life at home too hopelessly rigid to be longer endured. There is not a word in the text to justify the belief that her father loves her, apart from his own needs. She is expected to guard his gold and silver and to listen to his discussions with Tubal and Chus about the hated Antonio and his bond. So the girl must look after herself if she is to enjoy happiness in the future. Lorenzo knows that to allow Jessica to forsake her father and to rob him is a sin towards Heaven. He prays for punishment to be withheld because she has married a Christian, and, to his credit, it must be acknowledged that he is unconscious of any hypocrisy. As for the "braggart" Gratiano and the remaining Christians, we tolerate them because they love Antonio, the man who of all others most deserves our respect. Perhaps as Christians they insist too much on their moral superiority, but this is natural after Marlowe's play had been seen on the stage.

Of course, there are critics who will hold that Marlowe's Christians, in some respects, are more life-like than Shakespeare's. Perhaps if "The Merchant of Venice" had been written while Marlowe was alive, he would have challenged Shakespeare to uphold that in matters of conduct where money interests were involved there was any marked distinction between the morals of the believer and the unbeliever. Marlowe might have contended that out of one hundred Christians ninety-nine would act as his Governor of Malta had done, though he was a Knight of St. John. It might not be impossible for a Christian to persuade himself that money taken forcibly from the infidel Jew, as a tribute, could justly be withheld from the infidel Turk to whom it was due, and that it was folly to hesitate in cutting the cord that would let the infidel Jew into the burning cauldron, instead of the infidel Turk for whom it was designed, especially when one hundred thousand pounds of the citizens' money would in that way be saved. As a mere worldly truism the words that Barabas utters, when his daughter changes her faith, have a deeper significance than the "noble platitudes" of Lorenzo and Jessica:

> "She that varies from me in belief,
>   Gives great presumption that she loves me not ;
>   Or loving, does mislike of something done."

Shakespeare, probably, would have answered Marlowe's objection with the assurance that there still remained the odd Christian out of every hundred to be reckoned with, and that he himself was more interested in showing the world what men ought to be like than what they actually were. But if Shakespeare preferred to live outside the walls of reality, he did so only in imagination, for he must have had a very practical knowledge of men's dealings with each other. No doubt our great dramatist was not eager to break with conventions or to imitate Marlowe by saying unpalatable truths about the Christians at a time when he himself was still seeking the favour of Elizabeth's Court.

The Authors of " King Henry the Eighth."[*]

The play of " Henry VIII." first appeared in print in 1623, seven years after Shakespeare's death. It was published in the first collected edition of the poet's dramas, and so became known to the world as his play. For two centuries the genuineness of the drama was not called in question. The earliest commentators never expressed misgivings on the subject, nor is there evidence to show that Shakespeare's contemporaries disputed the authorship. Choice extracts from the play have appeared in collections of poetry, which compare favourably with selections from " Hamlet " or " Macbeth." Wolsey's famous soliloquy is universally thought to be Shakespeare's reflections on the vicissitudes of life. At the British Museum will be found versions of the play in French, German, Italian, and even one in Greek. The drama, moreover, is familiar to the playgoer, while eminent actors and actresses, with no intention of impersonating the creations of an inferior dramatist, have won distinction in the characters of the Cardinal and of Queen Katharine. Yet, in the face of evidence that is apparently convincing, it may be safely assumed that " Henry VIII." is not Shakespeare's play in the sense in which we speak of " Hamlet " or " Macbeth " as being his. Indeed, the statement has been put forth that not one line of the play was written by its reputed author.

Now it is always an ungrateful task to defend an argument which no one cares to accept, and the admirers of those scenes which have made actors and actresses famous, and of those speeches which

* *The New Age*, September 15, 1910.

adorn our books of extracts, are still too numerous and too enthusiastic to desire any other dramatist than Shakespeare to be the author of them. Possession is nine points of the law, and while tradition has the prior claim, public opinion will not readily endorse the verdict of a handful of literary sceptics. On the other hand, it must be conceded that even to challenge the genuineness of a play attributed to the world's greatest dramatist does involve, to some extent, a censure upon that play. The doubt implies that the play, as a whole, does not average the work of Shakespeare's later dramas, that it does not bear comparison with the " Winter's Tale," " Cymbeline," and the " Tempest," plays which, in the date of their composition, are contemporary with " Henry VIII.," and which were written at a time when the poet had obtained complete mastery over the resources of his art. If there are precedents of poets living till their once-glowing imaginations become cold, there is no record of a dramatist losing technical skill which has been acquired by the experience of a lifetime. It was but natural, then, that there should exist a feeling of uneasiness in the minds of impartial inquirers in regard to the authorship of this play, and it may be worth while to consider the history of the controversy.

The earliest known mention of the play is by a contemporary, Thomas Lorkin, in a letter of the last day of June, 1613. He writes that the day before, while Burbage and his company were playing " Henry VIII." in the Globe Theatre, the building was burnt down through a discharge of "chambers," that is to say of small pieces of cannon. Early in the month following Sir Henry Wotton writes to his nephew giving particulars of the fire, and describing the pageantry, which was evidently an important feature of the play:

> "The King's players had a new play called 'All is True,' representing some principal pieces of the reign of Henry the Eighth, which was set forth with many extraordinary circumstances of pomp and majesty, even to the matting of the stage; the Knights of the Order with their Georges and Garter, the guards with their embroidered coats, and the like; sufficient in truth, within a while, to make greatness very familiar if not ridiculous."

Now, if Sir Henry Wotton is correct in his assertion that the play was a *new* one in 1613, it was probably the last play written by Shakespeare: although some commentators contend that there is internal evidence to show that the play was written during Elizabeth's reign, and that after her death it was amended by the insertion of speeches complimentary to the new sovereign, King James. In 1623 the play appears in print inserted in the first collected edition of Shakespeare's dramas, by Heminge and Condell, who were the poet's fellow-actors, and who claim to have printed all the plays from the author's manuscripts. If, then, this statement were trustworthy, there could be no reason to doubt the genuineness of the drama. But the copies in the hands of Heminge and Condell were evidently in some cases very imperfect, either in consequence of the burning of the Globe Theatre, or by the necessary wear and tear of years. And it is certain that, in several instances, the editors reprinted the plays from the earlier quarto impressions with but few changes, sometimes for the better, and sometimes for the worse. It has also been ascertained that at least four of the plays in the folio were only partially written by Shakespeare, while no mention is made of his possible share in " Pericles," the play having been omitted altogether. So that it is presumed that if " Henry VIII.," in its present form, was a play rewritten by theatre-hacks to replace a similar play by Shakespeare that was destroyed in the fire, the editors would not be unlikely to insert it in the folio instead of the original.

So long as Shakespeare's authorship was not doubted there seems to have been no desire on the part of commentators to call attention to faults which are obvious to every careful reader of the play. Most of the early criticisms are confined to remarks on single scenes or speeches irrespective of the general character of the drama and its personages. Comments such as the following of Dr. Drake fairly represent those of most writers until the middle of the last century. He writes in 1817 : " The entire interest of the tragedy turns upon the characters of Queen Katherine and Cardinal Wolsey, the former being the finest picture of suffering and defenceless virtue, and the latter of disappointed ambition, that poet ever drew." Dr. Johnson, who ranks the play as second class among the historical works, had previously asserted " that the genius of Shakespeare comes in and goes out with Katherine. Every other part may be easily conceived and easily written."

When, however, the play is judged as a work of art in its complete form, the difficulty of writing favourably of its dramatic qualities becomes evident by the apologetic modes of expression used. Schlegel remarks that " Henry VIII." has somewhat " of a prosaic appearance, for Shakespeare, artist - like, adapted himself to the quality of his materials. While others of his works, both in elevation of fancy, and in energy of pathos and character tower far above this, we have here, on the other hand, occasion to admire his nice powers of discrimination and his perfect knowledge of courts and the world." Coleridge is content to define the play as that of "a sort of historical masque or show play"; and Victor Hugo observes that Shakespeare is so far English as to attempt to extenuate the failings of Henry VIII., adding, "it is true that the eye of Elizabeth is fixed upon him!"

In an interesting little volume containing the journal of Emily Shore, who made some valuable contributions to natural history, are to be found some remarks upon the play written in the year 1836. The criticism is the more noteworthy since Miss Shore was only in her sixteenth year when she wrote it, and she then showed no slight appreciation of literature, especially of Shakespeare:

"This evening my uncle finished reading 'King Henry VIII.' I must say I was mightily disappointed in it. Whether it is that I am not capable of understanding Shakespeare and cannot distinguish his beauties, I do not know. There is no effort in Shakespeare's works ; he takes so little pains that what is interesting or noble or sublime or finely exhibiting the features of the mind, seems to drop from his pen by chance. One cannot help thinking that every play is executed with slovenly neglect, that he has done himself injustice and that if he pleased he might have given to the world works which would throw into the shade all that he has actually written. To be sure this gives one a very exalted idea of his intellect, for even if the mere unavoidable overflowings of his genius excel the depths of other men's minds, how magnificent must have been the fountain of that genius whose very bubbles sparkle so beautifully! But to speak of 'Henry VIII.' in particular.

Henry himself, Katherine and Wolsey, though they display a degree of character, are not half so vigorously drawn as I had expected, or as I would methinks have done myself. The character of Cranmer exists more in Henry's language about him than in his own actions."

To come now to the opinion of the German commentators. Gervinus observes:

"No one in this short explanation of the main character of 'Henry VIII.' will mistake the certain hand of the poet. It is otherwise when we approach closer to the development of the action and attentively consider the poetic diction. The impression on the whole becomes then at once strange and unrefreshing; the mere external threads seem to be lacking which ought to link the actions to each other; the interest of the feelings becomes strangely divided, it is continually drawn into new directions and is nowhere satisfied. At first it clings to Buckingham, and his designs against Wolsey, but with the second act he leaves the stage; then Wolsey attracts our attention in an increased degree, and he, too, disappears in the third act; in the meanwhile our sympathies are more and more strongly drawn to Katherine, who then likewise leaves the stage in the fourth act; and after we have been thus shattered through four acts by circumstances of a purely tragic character, the fifth act closes with a merry festivity for which we are in no wise prepared, crowning the King's loose passion with victory in which we could take no warm interest."

Ulrici is even more severe in his remarks upon the play:

"The drama of 'Henry VIII.' is poetically untrue, devoid of real life, defective in symmetry and composition, because wanting in internal organic construction, *i.e.*, in ethical vitality."

So also is Professor Hertzberg:

"A chronicle history with three and a half catastrophes varied by a marriage and a coronation pageant, ending abruptly with the baptism of a child in which are combined the elements of a satirical drama with a prophetic ecstasy, and all this loosely connected by the nominal hero whom no poet in heaven or earth could ever have formed into a tragic character."

And Dr. Elze, who is a warm supporter of Shakespeare's authorship, admits that the play—

"measured by the standard of the historical drama is inferior to the other histories and wants both a grand historical substance and the unity of strictly defined dramatic structure."

But it is not only with the general design of the play and its feeble characterization that fault is found, but also with the versification. The earliest criticism on the peculiarity of the metre of the play appeared about 1757. It consists of some remarks, published by Mr. Thomas Edwards, which were made by Mr. Roderick on Warburton's edition of Shakespeare. Mr. Roderick, after pointing out that there are in the play many more lines than in any other which end with a redundant syllable, continues:

"This Fact (whatever Shakespeare's design was in it) is undoubtedly true, and may be demonstrated to Reason, and proved to sense; the first by comparing any number of lines in this Play, with an equal number in any other Play, by which it will appear that this Play has very near *two* redundant verses to *one* in any other Play. And to prove it to sense, let anyone read aloud an hundred lines in any other Play, and an hundred in this; and if he perceives not the tone and cadence of his own voice to be involuntarily altered in the latter case from what it was in the former, I would never advise him to give much credit to the information of his ears."

Later on we find that Emerson is also struck with the peculiarity of the metre, and in his lecture on " Representative Men," observes:

" In ' Henry VIII.' I think I see plainly the cropping out of the original rock on which his (Shakespeare's) own finer structure was laid. The first play was written by a superior thoughtful man, with a vicious ear. I can mark his lines and know well their cadence. See Wolsey's soliloquy, and the following scene with Cromwell, where, instead of the metre of Shakespeare, whose secret is that the thought constructs the tune, so that reading for

the sense will best bring out the rhythm ; here the lines are constructed on a given tune ; and the verse has even a trace of pulpit
eloquence."

Now these quotations, it may be urged, were
picked out with a view to prejudice a favourable
opinion of the play.   But disparagements are, none
the less, important links in a question of authorship.
In fact it was because Shakespearian critics, of un-
disputed authority, declared that " Henry VIII."
was not a play worthy of the poet's genius that a
few advanced scholars were encouraged to come
forward and pronounce that no part of the play had
been written by Shakespeare.

In the autumn of 1850 Mr. Spedding, the able editor
of Bacon's works, published a paper in the *Gentleman's Magazine* in which he stated it to be his belief
that a great portion of the play of " Henry VIII."
was written by Fletcher ; a conjecture that indeed
had been anticipated and was at once confirmed
by other writers.   Tennyson, on Mr. Spedding's
authority, had pointed out many years previously
the resemblance of the style in some parts of the
play to Fletcher's.   In fact, the conclusion arrived
at by the advanced critics was that the play has two
totally different metres which are the work of two
different authors.   On this point Mr. Spedding
wrote :

" A distinction so broad and so uniform running through so
large a portion of the same piece cannot have been accidental,
and the more closely it is examined, the more clearly will it
appear that the metre in these two sets of scenes is managed
upon entirely different principles and bears evidence of different
workmen."

This conclusion, however, was not endorsed by all commentators. It was acknowledged that metrical evidence must not be neglected, and that "there is no play of Shakespeare's in which eleven syllable lines are so frequent as they are in "Henry VIII.";" and even Swinburne, whose faith in Shakespeare's authorship was unwavering, asserted "that if not the partial work it may certainly be taken as the general model of Fletcher, in some not unimportant passages." It was contended besides that the poet's hand was hampered by a difficulty inherent in the subject, since of all Shakespeare's plays, "Henry VIII." is the nearest in its story to the poet's own time, and that the elliptical construction and the licence of versification, which are peculiar to this play, are necessary in order to bring the dialogue closer to the language of common life. In fact, Mr. Spedding's opponents, while admitting an anonymous hand in the prologue and epilogue, rejected the theory as to the manner in which the collaboration was carried out, and asserted that the structure of the play, the development of the action and the characters showed it to be the work of one hand, and that Shakespeare's.

Another challenger of the metre was Mr. Robert Boyle, who endeavoured to show, from a careful and elaborate study of Elizabethan blank verse, that Shakespeare had no share whatever in the composition of the play, and that whoever was the author who collaborated with Fletcher (in Mr. Boyle's opinion it was Massinger) he certainly did not write before 1612, for the metrical peculiarities of the verse are those of the later dramatic style, of which the earliest characteristics did not make themselves felt in the work of any poet till about 1607. It was after reading this paper that Robert Browning, then the president of the New Shakspere Society, wrote his final judgment on the play which was published in the Society's "Transactions."

"As you desired I have read once again 'Henry the Eighth'; my opinion about the scanty portion of Shakespeare's authorship in it was formed about fifty years ago, while ignorant of any evidence external to the text itself. I have little doubt now that Mr. Boyle's judgment is right altogether; that the original play, presumably Shakespeare's, was burnt along with the Globe Theatre; that the present work is a substitution for it, probably with certain reminiscences of 'All is true.' In spite of such huff-and-bullying as Charles Knight's for example, I see little that transcends the power of Massinger and Fletcher to execute. It is very well to talk of the tediousness of the Chronicles, which have furnished pretty well whatever is admirable in the characters of Wolsey and Katherine; as wisely should we depreciate the bone which holds the marrow we enjoy on a toast. The versification is nowhere Shakespeare's. But I have said my little say for what it is worth."

There is yet another peculiarity that is special to this play, and it is one which seems to have escaped the notice of the critics. The stage-directions in it are unlike those of any other play published in the first folio. In no other play are they so full, and so carefully detailed. With the exception of "Henry VIII.," the stage-directions in the folio are so few in number and so abbreviated that they appear to have been written solely for the author's convenience. It is very rare that any reference is made to movement, more than to indicate the entrance or exit of characters, or to note that they fight or that they die. Sometimes the characters are not so much as named, and the direction is simply, "Enter the French Power and the English

Lords "; at other times the directions are so concise
as to be almost incomprehensible to the modern
reader, for example, "Enter Hermione (like a
statue)," "Enter Imogene (in her bed)"! The
legitimate inference, therefore, is that Shakespeare
considered it to be no part of his business to be
explicit in these matters. It is startling, then, to
find, in the play of "Henry VIII.," a stage-direction
so elaborate as the following: "The Queen makes
no answer, rises out of her chair, goes about the
Court, comes to the King, and kneels at his feet,
then speaks." No doubt in Elizabeth's time all
stage movement was of the simplest kind, and of a
conventional order, so as to be applicable to a great
variety of plays, and what was special to any
particular play in the way of movement would, in
Shakespeare's dramas, be explained at rehearsal by
the author. So that the detailed and minute stage-
directions that in the first folio are special to
"Henry VIII." would seem to suggest that the play
was written at a time when the author was absent
from the theatre. To the actor, however, who is
experienced in the technicalities of the stage, these
elaborate directions show that the author was not
only very familiar with what in theatrical parlance
is known as stage "business," but that he regarded
the minute description of the actors' movements as
forming an essential part of the dramatist's duty.
In fact, the story of the play is made subservient
to the "business" or to pageant throughout. A
dramatic incident, then a procession, another
dramatic incident, and then another procession.
This seems to be the sort of effect aimed at. Towards
the year 1610 the taste for spectacle created by the

genius of Inigo Jones spread from the Court to the public theatre. Perhaps this may account for Shakespeare's early retirement. He wrote plays and not masques, and his genius lay in portraying the drama of human life. Unlike Ben Jonson, he never devoted his talents to the service of the stage carpenter. Seeing the altered condition of the public taste, there would be nothing unnatural in his yielding his place silently and without bitterness to others who were willing to supply the theatrical market with the desired commodity. Had Shakespeare wanted money it would perhaps be difficult to deny that he would have adapted his work to the requirement of the times. But by 1610 he was very well able to live in retirement upon a competent income, and it is difficult to believe that one who had attained his wonderful balance of intellect and heart, of reason and imagination, would have condescended to elaborate the details of baptismal and coronation festivities.

And now in conclusion, what is there to be said for or against the genuineness of the play? The supporters of the Shakespearian authorship dwell upon the beauty of particular passages, and on the general similarity, in many scenes, to Shakespeare's verse in his later plays; the sceptics contend that it is a mistake to leave entirely out of view the most important part of every drama—viz., its action and its characterization; and unreasonable, moreover, to suppose that Shakespeare had no imitators at the close of his successful career. But, say the admirers, this kind of reasoning is no evidence that Shakespeare was not the author of all that is most liked in the play. Here, however, we are met with

the argument that the popular scenes of all others
in the play, are those the most easily to be identified
with the metre peculiar to Fletcher. Then, again, it
is hardly possible to accept the opinion of Charles
Knight, Professor Delius, and Dr. Elze that all the
shortcomings of the play, both in the structure and
versification, are due to the fact that the poet was
hampered by a " difficulty inherent in the subject."
Is genius ever hampered by its subject ? Does not
history prove the contrary ? Have not the shackles
put upon musicians, poets, painters, and sculptors
by their patrons, instead of checking their genius,
elicited the most exquisite products of their imagination ? The conscientious inquirer, therefore, who
wades through a mass of literary criticism in the
hope of obtaining some elucidation of the question,
seems only doomed to experience disappointment.
Nothing is gained but an unsettling of all pre-
conceived ideas. If expectations of a possible
solution are aroused they are not fulfilled because
the unprejudiced mind refuses to accept conjectural
criticism and to believe more than it is possible to
know. Still, it must be admitted that in re-reading
the play in the light of all the more modern criticism
upon it, the dissatisfaction with the inferior portions
becomes more acute, while the finer scenes shine
with a lessened glory. It is not only dramatic
perception in the development of character that is
wanting, but the power which gives words form
and meaning is also lacking; the closely packed
expression, the lifelike reality and freshness, the
rapid and abrupt turnings of thought, so quick
that language can hardly follow fast enough ; the
impatient audacity of intellect and fancy with which

we are familiar in Shakespeare's later plays are not to be found in " Henry VIII." We miss even the objections raised by modern grammarians, the idle conceits, the play upon words, the puns, the improbability, the extravagance, the absurdity, the obscenity, the puerility, the bombast, the emphasis, the exaggeration. Therefore it must be admitted that in order to uphold " Henry VIII." as a late play of Shakespeare's, it becomes necessary for his sincere admirers to invent all sorts of apologies for its faults, and to overlook the consistent development of the poet's genius from the close of the great tragedies to the play of the " Tempest," " where we see him shining to the last in a steady, mild, unchanging glory."

TROILUS AND CRESSIDA*

The mystery in which the history of this play is shrouded bewilders students, for the information available is scanty. The play was entered on the *Stationers' Register* on February 7, 1603, as " The Booke of Troilus and Cresseda," but it was not to be printed until the publisher had got the necessary permission from its owners ; and it was also the same book, " as it *is* acted by my Lord Chamberlen's men," and a play of Shakespeare's had never before been entered on the *Register* as one that was being acted at the time of its publication, plays being seldom printed in those days until they had become, to some extent, obsolete on the stage. Then Mr. A. W. Pollard points out that the Globe managers often got some publisher to enter a play on the

* *The New Age*, November 28, 1912.

Stationers' Register in order to protect their play-house copies from pirates, and for this or some other reason not yet fully explained, the play did not get printed. But on January 28, 1609, another firm of publishers entered on the *Register* a book with a similar name, which soon afterwards was published, with the following words on its title-page: " The Historie of Troylus and Cresseda. As it *was* acted by the Kings Majesties servants at the 'Globe.'" Shortly afterwards this title-page was suppressed, being torn out of the book, and another one inserted to allow of the following qualification : " The Famous Historie of Troylus and Cresseid. Excellently expressing the beginning of their loves, with the conceited wooing of Pandarus, Prince of Licia." On both title-pages Shakespeare is announced as the author, and apparently the object of the second title-page was to contradict the former statement that the play had been acted at the Globe, or, in other words, was the property of the Globe managers ; and also to suggest by the title " Prince of Licia" that the book was not the same play as the one the actors of the theatre owned. In addition to the altered title there appeared on the back of the new leaf a preface, and this was another unusual proceeding, since there had not appeared before one attached to a Shakespeare play. No further editions were issued until 1623, when Heminge and Condell published their player's copy, with additions and corrections taken from the 1609 quarto. It was inserted in the first folio in a position between the Histories and Tragedies, where it appears unpaged after having been removed from its original position among the Tragedies. No mention is made of it in the contents of the volume. In the folio the play is called a tragedy, which, if a correct title, is not the one given to it in the 1609 preface.

Now, in the Epilogue to " Henry IV., Part Two," we have this allusion to a recently acted play by Shakespeare, which had not been well received by the audience, " Be it known to you, as it is very well, I was lately here in the end of a displeasing play, to pray your patience for it and to promise you a better. I meant, indeed, to pay you with this." And in 1903 Mr. Arthur Acheson, of Chicago, in his book on "Shakespeare and the Rival Poet," advanced the theory (1) that this " displeasing play," was " Troilus and Cressida"; (2) that it was written at some time between the autumn of 1598 and the spring of 1599; (3) that it preceded and did not follow Ben Jonson's " Poetaster," and therefore had nothing to do with the " War of the Theatres"; (4) that it was written to ridicule Chapman's fulsome praise of Homer and his Greek heroes—praise which was displayed in his prefaces to the seven books of the Iliad issued in that year. On this point Mr. Acheson says, forcibly:

" Chapman claims supremacy for Homer, not only as a poet, but as a moralist, and extends his claims for moral altitude to include the heroes of his epics. Shakespeare divests the Greek heroes of the glowing, but misty, nimbus of legend and mythology, and presents them to us in the light of common day, and as men in a world of men. In a modern Elizabethan setting he pictures these Greeks and Trojans, almost exactly as they appear in the sources from which he works. He does not stretch the truth of what he finds, nor draw wilfully distorted pictures, and yet, the Achilles, the Ulysses, the Ajax, etc., which we find in the play, have lost their demigodlike pose. How does he do it? The masterly realistic and satirical effect he produces comes wholly from a changed point of view. He displays pagan Greek and

Trojan life in action—with its low ideals of religion, womanhood, and honour, with its bloodiness and sensuality—upon a background from which he has eliminated historical perspective."

Nor is this explanation inapplicable when we realize how exaggerated are Chapman's eulogies on Homer. To take as an instance the following passage :

"Soldiers shall never spende their idle howres more profitablie then with his studious and industrious perusell ; in whose honors his deserts are infinite. Counsellors have never better oracles then his lines ; fathers have no morales so profitable for their children as his counsailes ; nor shal they ever give them more honord injunctions then to learne Homer without book, that being continually conversant in him his height may descend to their capacities, and his substance prove their worthiest riches. Husbands, wives, lovers, friends, and allies, having in him mirrors for all their duties ; all sortes of which concourse and societie, in other more happy ages, have in steed of sonnets and lascivious ballades, sung his Iliades."

Now, Mr. Acheson may be right as to the date in which "Troilus and Cressida" was written, because neither in its dramatic construction nor in its verse and characterization can the play consistently be called a later composition, so that it is possible to contend that the whole of the play, with the exception, perhaps, of the prologue, was written before "Henry IV., Part Two." It can be urged, also, that Ben Jonson's "Poetaster," which was acted in 1601, contains allusions to Shakespeare's play, and to its having been unfavourably received ; then that certain incidents in the life of Essex come into the play, and that these would not have been mentioned had the play been written later than the spring of 1599, when Essex had left for Ireland.

With regard to the "Poetaster," it is now generally admitted that there is no evidence to support the assertion that, at the time this satirical play was written, its author was on bad terms with Shakespeare. In it Jonson announced his next production to be a tragedy, and in 1603 "Sejanus" followed at the Globe; Shakespeare was in the cast, and may have been also a collaborator. But the failure of this tragedy to please the patrons of the Globe may have led to a temporary estrangement from that theatre, for Jonson did not undervalue himself or forget that Chapman, as Mr. Acheson has clearly shown, was always a bitter opponent of Shakespeare, while it was characteristic of Jonson himself to be equally ready to defend or to quarrel with friends. Now in the "Poetaster" Jonson refers to Chapman and to his "divine" Homer, as, for instance, when he makes the father of Ovid say: "Ay, your god of poets there, whom all of you admire and reverence so much, Homer, he whose worm-eaten statue must not be spewed against but with hallowed lips and grovelling adoration, what was he? What was he? . . . You'll tell me his name shall live; and that, now being dead, his works have eternized him and made him divine" (Act I., Scene 1.) Again, the incident of the gods' banquet, although it is modelled by Ben Jonson upon the synod of the Iliad, is obviously a satire upon Chapman's ecstatic admiration for Homer's heroes. It may also refer to Shakespeare's "Troilus and Cressida," for if this comedy was acted in 1598 it might well have been suppressed after its first performance, since to the groundlings it must have been "caviare," and to Chapman's allies, the scholars, a malicious piece of "ignorance and impiety," while the Court would have been sure to take offence at the Essex incidents. Besides Jonson, in the

"Poetaster," seems to be defending someone from attacks who has dared to laugh at Chapman's idol. This appears in such witty expressions as "Gods may grow impudent in iniquity, and they must not be told of it" . . . "So now we may play the fool by authority" . . . "What, shall the king of gods turn the king of good fellows, and have no fellow in wickedness? This makes our poets that know our profaneness live as profane as we" (Act IV., Scene 3.) Continually in this play is Jonson attacking Chapman for the same reason that Shakespeare did, and, more than this, Jonson proclaims that the poet Virgil is as much entitled to be regarded "divine" as Homer, while the word "divine" is seized hold of for further satire in the remark, "Well said, my divine deft Horace."

Jonson says he wrote his "Poetaster" to ridicule Marston, the dramatist, who previously had libelled him on the stage. In addition to Marston, Jonson appeared himself in the play as Horace, together with Dekker and other men in the theatre. It was but natural, then, for commentators to centre their attention on those parts of the play where Marston and Horace were prominent. But there is an underplot to which very little attention hitherto has been given, and it is hardly likely, if Jonson was writing a comedy in order to satirize living persons and contemporary events, that his underplot would be altogether free from topical allusions. It may be well, then, to relate the story of the underplot, and, if possible, to try to show its significance. Julia, who is Cæsar's daughter, lives at Court, and she invites to the palace her lover, Ovid, a merchant's son, and some tradesmen of the town, with their wives; then she contrives, unknown to her father, for these plebeians to counterfeit the gods at a banquet prepared for them.   An actor of the Globe reports to one of Cæsar's spies that Julia has sent to the playhouse to borrow suitable properties for this "divine" masquerade, so that while the sham gods are in the midst of their licentious convivialities Cæsar suddenly appears, led there by his spy, and is horrified at the daring act of profanity perpetrated by his daughter.   "Be they the gods!" he exclaims,

> "Oh impious sight ! . . .
>   Profaning thus their dignities in their forms,
>   And making them like you but counterfeits."

Then he goes on to say :

> " If you think gods but feigned and virtue painted,
>   Know *we* sustain our actual residence,
>   And with the title of our emperor
>   Retain his spirit and imperial power."

And then, with correct imperial conventionality, he proceeds to punish the offenders, locking up his daughter behind "iron doors" and exiling her lover. Now, Horace—that is to say, Jonson—is supposed by the revellers to be responsible for having betrayed the inspirer of these antics.   But this implication Jonson indignantly repudiates in a scene between Horace, the spy, and the Globe player, in which Horace severely upbraids them for their malice :

> " To prey upon the life of innocent mirth
>   And harmless pleasures bred of noble wit,"

a rebuke that found expression in almost similar words in the 1609 preface to Shakespeare's "Troilus and Cressida": "For it is a birth of (that) brain that never undertook anything comical vainly : and were but the vain names of comedies changed for titles of commodities or of plays for pleas, you should see all those grand censors that now style them such vanities flock to them for the main grace of their gravities." Now Jonson, if he, indeed, intended to defend the attacks made on his friend Shakespeare's play, has shown considerable adroitness in the delicate task he undertook, for since the "Poetaster" was written to be acted at the Blackfriars, a theatre under Court patronage, Jonson could not there abuse "the grand censors," and this he avoids doing by making Cæsar justly incensed at the impudence of the citizens in daring to counterfeit the divine gods, while Horace, out of reach of Cæsar's ear, soundly rates the police spy and the actor for mistaking the shadow for the substance and regarding playacting as if it were political conspiracy.   But what, it may be contended, connects the underplot in the "Poetaster" directly with Shakespeare's play is the speech of citizen Mercury and its satirical insistence that immorality may be tolerated by the gods :

"The great god Jupiter, of his licentious goodness, willing to make this feast no fast from any manner of pleasure, nor to bind any god or goddess to be anything the more god or goddess for their names, he gives them all free licence to speak no wiser than persons of baser titles ; and to be nothing better than common men or women.   And, therefore, no god shall need to keep himself more strictly to his goddess than any man does to his wife ; nor any goddess shall need to keep herself more strictly to her god than any woman does to her husband.   But since it is no part of wisdom in these days to come into bonds, it should be lawful for every lover to break loving oaths, to change their lovers, and make love to others, as the heat of everyone's blood and the spirit of our nectar shall inspire.   And Jupiter save Jupiter !"

Now this speech, it may be contended, is but a good-natured parody of Shakespeare's travesty of the Iliad story, as he wrote it in answer to Chapman's absurd claim for the sanctity of Homer's characters. Shakespeare's consciousness of power might naturally have incited him to place himself immediately by the side of Homer, but it is more likely that he was interested in the ethical than in the personal point of view. Unlike most of his plays, as Dr. Ward has pointed out, this comedy follows no single original source accurately, because the author's satire was more topical than anything he had previously attempted, except, perhaps, in "Love's Labour's Lost." But Shakespeare for once had miscalculated not his own powers, but the powers of the "grand censors," who could suppress plays which reflected upon the morality or politics of those who moved in high places; nor had he sufficiently allowed for the hostility of the "sinners who lived in the suburbs." Shakespeare, indeed, found one of the most striking compositions of his genius disliked and condemned not from its lack of merit, but for reasons that Jonson so forcibly points out in words put into the mouth of Virgil:

> "'Tis not the wholesome sharp morality,
>   Or modest anger of a satiric spirit,
>   That hurts or wounds the body of the state;
>   But the sinister application
>   Of the malicious, ignorant, and base
>   Interpreter, who will distort and strain
>   The general scope and purpose of an author
>   To his particular and private spleen."

The stigma that rested on Shakespeare in his lifetime for having written this play rests on him still, for some unintelligible reason, since no man ever sat down to put his thoughts on paper with a loftier motive. But so it is! Then, as now, whenever a dramatist attempts to be teacher and preacher, all the other teachers and preachers in the world hold up their hands in horror and exclaim: " What impiety! What stupendous ignorance!"

Gervinus, in his criticism of this play, compares the satire of the Elizabethen poet with that of Aristophanes, and points out that the Greek dramatist directed his sallies against the living. This, he contends, should ever be the object of satire, because a man must not war against the defenceless and dead. Yet Shakespeare's instincts as a dramatist were too unerring for him to be unconscious of this fundamental principle of his art. The stage in his time supplied the place now occupied by the Press, and political discussions were carried on in public through the mouth of the actor, of which few indications can now be traced on the printed page, owing to the difficulty of fitting the date of composition with that of the performance. Heywood, the dramatist, in his answer to the Puritan's abuse of the theatre, alludes to the stage as the great political schoolmaster of the people. And yet until recent years the labours of commentators have been chiefly confined to making literary comparisons, to discovering sources of plots, and the origin of expressions, so that there still remains much investigation needed to discover Shakespeare's political, philosophical, and religious affinities as they appear reflected in his plays. Mr. Richard

Simpson, the brilliant Shakespearian scholar, many years ago pointed out the necessity for a new departure in criticism, and added that it was still thought derogatory to Shakespeare "to make him an upholder of any principles worth assertion," or to admit that, as a reasoner, he took any decided part in the affairs which influenced the highest minds of his day. Now, in regard to politics, government by factions was then the prevailing feature; factions consisting of individuals who centred round some nobleman, whom the Queen favoured and made, or weakened, according to her judgment or caprice. In the autumn of 1597 Essex's influence over the Queen was waning, and after a sharp rebuke received from her at the Privy Council table, he abruptly left the Court and sullenly withdrew to his estate at Wanstead, where he remained so long in retirement that his friends remonstrated with him against his continued absence. One of them, who signed himself "Thy true servant not daring to subscribe," urged him to attend every Council and to let nothing be settled either at home or abroad without his knowledge. He should stay in the Court, and perform all his duties there, where he can make a greater show of discontent than he possibly could being absent; there is nothing, adds this writer, that his enemies so much wish, enjoy, and rejoice in as his absence. He is advised not to sue any more, "because necessity will entreat for him." All he need do now is to dissemble like a courtier, and show himself outwardly unwilling of that which he has inwardly resolved. For by retiring he is playing his enemies' game, since "the greatest subject that ever is or was greatest, in the prince's favour, in his absence is not missed." In "Troilus and Cressida" we have a similar situation, and we hear similar advice given. Achilles, like Essex, has withdrawn unbidden and discontentedly to his tent, refusing to come again to his general's council table. For doing so Ulysses remonstrates with him in almost the same words as the writer of the anonymous letter.

> " The present eye praises the present object.
> Then marvel not, thou great and complete man,
> That all the Greeks begin to worship Ajax ;
> Since things in motion sooner catch the eye
> Than what not stirs.   The cry went once on thee,
> And still it might, and yet it may again,
> If thou would'st not entomb thyself alive,
> And case thy reputation in thy tent ;
> Whose glorious deeds, but in these fields of late,
> Made emulous missions 'mongst the gods themselves
> And drave great Mars to faction."

Then Achilles replies :

> " Of this my privacy I have strong reasons."

And Ulysses continues :

> " But 'gainst your privacy
> The reasons are more potent and heroical,
> 'Tis known, Achilles, that you are in love
> With one of Priam's daughters."
> ACHILLES : Ha ! known ?
> ULYSSES : Is that a wonder ?
>
> *   *   *   *   *
>
> All the commerce that you have had with Troy
> As perfectly is ours as yours, my lord ;
> And better would it fit Achilles much
> To throw down Hector than Polyxena."

If, again, we turn to the life and letters of Essex, we find there that upon the 11th of February, 1598, "it is spied out by some that my Lord of Essex is again fallen in love with his fairest B.: it cannot chance but come to her Majesty's ears, and then he is undone." The lady in question was Mary Brydges, a maid-of-honour and celebrated beauty. Again, in the same month Essex writes to the Queen, "I was never proud till your Majesty sought to make me too base." And Achilles is blamed by Agamemnon for his pride in a remarkably fine passage. Then after news had come of the disaster to the Queen's troops in Ireland, in the summer of 1598, Essex reminds the Queen that, "I posted up and first offered my attendance after my poor advice to your Maj. But your Maj. rejected both me and my letter: the cause, as I hear, was that I refused to give counsel when I was last called to my Lord Keeper." A similar situation is found in the play. Agamemnon sends for Achilles to attend the Council and he refuses to come, and later on, when he desires a reconciliation, the Council pass him by unnoticed. It is almost impossible to read the third act of this play without being reminded of these and other incidents in Essex's life. Nor would Shakespeare forget the stir that had been created in London when in 1591 it was known at Court that Essex, at the siege of Rouen, had sent a personal challenge to the governor of the town couched in the following words: "Si vous voulez combattre vous-même à cheval ou à pied je maintiendrai que la querelle du rois est plus juste que celle de la ligue, et que ma Maîtresse est plus belle que la votre." And Æneas, the Trojan, brings a challenge in almost identical words from Hector to the Greeks. It is true that this incident is in the Iliad together with the incidents connected with the withdrawal of Achilles, but Shakespeare selected his material from many sources and appears to have chosen what was most likely to appeal to his audience.   Now it is not presumed that Achilles is Essex, nor that Ajax is Raleigh, nor Agamemnon Elizabeth, or that Shakespeare's audience for a moment supposed that they were; although it is to be noticed that the Achilles who comes into Shakespeare's play is not the same man at the beginning and end of the play as he is in the third act, where, in conversation with Ulysses he suddenly becomes an intelligent being and not simply a prize-fighter.   To the injury of his drama, Shakespeare here runs away from his Trojan story, and does so for reasons that must have been special to the occasion for which the play was written.   For about this time, the Privy Council wrote to some Justices of the Peace in Middlesex, complaining that certain players at the Curtain were reported to be representing upon the stage "the persons of some gentlemen of good descent and quality that are yet alive," and that the actors were impersonating these aristocrats " under obscure manner, but yet in such sorte as all the hearers may take notice of the matter and the persons that are meant thereby.   This being a thing very unfit and offensive."   The protest seems almost to suggest that the Achilles's scenes in Shakespeare's play express, " under obscure manner," reflections upon contemporary politicians.   But, indeed, the growing political unrest which marked the last few years of Elizabeth's reign could not fail to find expression on the stage.

It must be remembered, besides, that the years 1597 to 1599 were marked by a group of dramas which may be called plays of political adventure. Nash had got into trouble over a performance of "The Isle of Dogs" at the Rose in 1597. In the same year complaints were made against Shakespeare for putting Sir John Oldcastle on the stage in the character of Falstaff. Also at the same period Shakespeare's "Richard the Second" was published, but not without exciting suspicions at Court, for the play had a political significance in the eyes of Catholics. Queen Mary of Scotland told her English judges that "she remembered they had done the same to King Richard, whom they had degraded from all honour and dignity." Then on the authority of Mr. H. C. Hart we are told that Ben Jonson brought Sir Walter Raleigh, the best hated man in England, on to the stage in the play of "Every Man Out of His Humour," in 1599, and, as a consequence, in the summer of the same year it was decided by the Privy Council that restrictions should be placed on satires, epigrams, and English histories, and that "noe plays be printed except they be allowed by such as have an authoritie." Dramatists, therefore, had to be much more circumspect in their political allusions after 1599 than they were before.

There are two new conjectures therefore put forward in this article : (1) That the underplot in the "Poetaster" contains allusions to Shakespeare's play, and (2) that the withdrawal of Achilles is a reflection on the withdrawal of Essex from Elizabeth's Court. Presuming that further evidence may one day be found to support these suppositions, it is worth while to consider them in relation to the history of the play.

And first to clear away the myth in connection with the idea that this is one of Shakespeare's late plays, or that it was only partly written by the poet, or written at different periods of his life. It may be confidently asserted that Shakespeare allowed no second hand to meddle with a work so personal to himself as this one, nor was he accustomed to seek the help of any collaborator in a play that he himself initiated. We know, besides, that he wrote with facility and rapidly. As to the date of the play, the evidence of the loose dramatic construction, and the preference for dialogue where there should be drama, place it during the period when Shakespeare was writing his histories. The grip that he ultimately obtained over the stage handling of a story so as to produce a culminating and overpowering impression on his audience is wanting in "Troilus and Cressida." In fact, it is impossible to believe that this play was written after "Julius Cæsar," "Much Ado," or "Twelfth Night." Nor is there evidence of revision in the play, since there are no topical allusions to be found in it which point to a later date than 1598 except perhaps in the prologue, which could hardly have been written before 1601, and did not appear in print before 1623. Again, it is contended that there is too much wisdom crammed into the play to allow of its being an early composition. But the false ethics underlying the Troy story, which Shakespeare meant to satirize in "Troilus and Cressida," had been previously exposed in his poem of "Lucrece":

> "Show me the strumpet that began this stir,
> That with my nails her beauty I may tear.
> Thy heat of lust, fond Paris, did incur

8

This load of wrath that burning Troy did bear :
Thy eye kindled the fire that burneth here ;
    And here in Troy, for trespass of thine eye
    The sire, the son, the dame, and daughter die.

"Why should the private pleasure of some one
Become the public plague of many moe ?
Let sin, alone committed, light alone
Upon his head that hath transgressed so ;
Let guiltless souls be freed from guilty woe :
    For one's offence why should so many fall,
    To plague a private sin in general.

"Lo, here weeps Hecuba, here Priam dies,
Here manly Hector faints, here Troilus swounds,
Here friend by friend in bloody charnel lies,
And friend to friend gives unadvisèd wounds,
And one man's lust these many lives confounds ;
    Had doting Priam check'd his son's desire,
    Troy had been bright with fame, and not with fire."

The difficulty with commentators is the knowledge that the play might have been written yesterday, while the treatment of the subject, in its modernity, is as far removed from "The Tempest" as it is from "Henry V." Now, if the drama be recognized as a satire written under provocation and with extraordinary mental energy, the date of the composition can be as well fixed for 1598, when Shakespeare was thirty-four years old, as for the year 1609. There is, besides, something to be said with regard to its vocabulary, as Mr. Richard Simpson has shown, which is peculiar to this play alone. Shakespeare introduces into it a large number of new words which he had never used before and never employed afterwards. The list is a long one. There are 126 latinized words that are coined or used only for this play, words such as propugnation, protractive, Ptisick, publication, cog-

nition, commixture, commodious, community, com-
plimental. And in addition to all the latinized
words there are 124 commoner words simple and
compound, not elsewhere to be found in the poet's
plays, showing an unwonted search after verbal
novelty.

We will now, with the help of the new information,
attempt to unravel the mystery as to the history of
the play. The creation of the character of Falstaff
in "Henry IV." (Part I.) brought Shakespeare's
popularity, as a dramatist, to its zenith, and he
seized the opportunity to reply to the attacks made
upon himself, as a poet, by his rival poet, Chapman,
and wrote a play giving a modern interpretation to
the story of Troy, and working into the underplot
some political allusion to Essex and the Court. The
play may have been acted at the Curtain late in
1598, or at the Globe in the spring of 1599, or,
perhaps, privately at some nobleman's mansion,
who might have been one of Essex's faction. It was
not liked, and Shakespeare experienced his first and
most serious reverse on the stage. But he quickly
retrieved his position by producing another Falstaff
play, "Henry IV." (Part II.), in the summer of 1599,
followed by "Henry V." in the same autumn, when
Essex's triumphs in Ireland are predicted. Shakespeare, none the less, must have felt both grieved
and annoyed by the treatment his satirical comedy
had received from the hands of the "grand censors."
So at Christmas, 1601, when Ben Jonson produced
his "Poetaster" at Blackfriars, the younger
dramatist defended his friend from the silly objections which had been made to the Trojan comedy.
Then early in 1603 a revival of "Troilus and

Cressida " may have been contemplated at the
Globe, and also its publication, but the death of
Essex was still too near to the memory of Londoners
to make this possible, and the suggestion may have
been dropped on the eve of its fulfilment; Shakespeare, meanwhile, had written a prologue, to be
spoken by an actor in armour, in imitation of
Jonson's prologue, with a view to protect his play
from further hostility.   In 1609 Shakespeare was
preparing to give up his connection with the stage,
and may have handed his copy of the play to some
publishers, for a consideration, and the book was
then printed. The Globe players, however, demurred
and claimed the property as theirs.   The publishers
then removed their first title page and inserted
another one to give the appearance to the reader of
the play being new.   They also wrote a preface
to show that the publication, if unauthorized, was
warranted, since the play had not been acted on
the *public* stage.   The real object of the preface,
however, was to defend the play from the attacks of
the " grand censors," who thought that the comedy
had some deep political significance, and was not
merely intended to amuse and instruct.   It also
shows the writer's resentment at the high-handed
action of the " grand possessors," the Globe players,
who were unwilling either to act the play themselves or yet to allow it to be published.

III

SOME STAGE VERSIONS

"THE MERCHANT OF VENICE."
"ROMEO AND JULIET."
"HAMLET."
"KING LEAR."

III

SOME STAGE VERSIONS

A CRITICAL and genuine appreciation of the poet's work imposes a reverence for the constructive plan as well as for the text. Why should a Shakespeare, whose cunning hand divined the dramatic sequence of his story, have it improved by a modern playwright or actor-manager? The answer will be: Because the modern experts are familiar with theatrical effects of a kind Shakespeare never lived to see. But if a modern rearrangement of Shakespeare's plays is necessary to suit these theatrical effects, the question may well be discussed as to whether rearrangements with all their modern advantages are of more dramatic value than the perfect work of the master.

Among all innovations on the stage, perhaps the most far-reaching in its effect on dramatic construction was the act-drop. Elizabethan dramatists had to round off a scene to a conclusion, for there was no kindly curtain to cover retreat from a deadlock. The art of modern play-writing is to arrest the action suddenly upon a thrilling situation, and leave the characters between the horns of a dilemma. At a critical moment the act-drop comes down; and after the necessary interval goes up again, showing that the characters have in the meantime somehow got out of the difficulty. This leaves much to the fancy, but does not feed the imagination. This leading up to a terminal climax, a "curtain," is but the appetite for the feast, and not the food itself. It assumes that the palate of the audience is depraved in its taste, and that it is one for which the best work is perhaps not best suited; but it is a form of art, and plays can be written after this form, and well written. Apart, however, from the question as to the theatrical gain of such a crude device as a "curtain," Shakespeare wrote with consummate art to show the tide of human affairs, its flow and its ebb, and his constructive plan is particularly unsuited to the act-drop. Upon one of Shakespeare's plays the curtain falls like the knife of a guillotine, and the effect is similar to ending a piece of music abruptly at its highest note, simply for the sake of creating some startling impression.

The way in which some modern managers, both here and in America, set about producing a play of Shakespeare's seems to be as follows : Choose your play, and be sure to note carefully in what country the incidents take place. Having done this, send artists to the locality to make sketches of the country, of its streets, its houses, its landscape, of its people, and of their costumes. Tell your artists that they must accurately reproduce the colouring of the sky, of the foliage, of the evening shadows, of the moonlight, of the men's hair and the women's eyes ; for all these details are important to the proper understanding of Shakespeare's play. Send, moreover, your leading actor and actress to spend some weeks in the neighbourhood that they may become acquainted with the manners, the gestures, the emotions of the residents, for these things also are necessary to the proper understanding of the play. Then, when you have collected, at vast expense, labour, and research, this interesting information about a country of which Shakespeare was possibly entirely ignorant, thrust all this extraneous knowledge into your representation, whether it fit the context or not; let it justify the rearrangement of your play, the crowding of your stage with supernumeraries, the addition of incidental songs and glees, to say nothing of inappropriateness of costume and misconception of character, until the play, if it does not cease to be intelligible or consistent, thrives only by virtue of its imperishable vitality, or by its strength of characterization, and by its brilliancy of dialogue.

These are but a few of the inconsistencies consequent upon the rage for foisting foreign local colour into a Shakespearian play. But if the same amount of industry bestowed in ascertaining the manners and customs of foreign countries had been spent in acquiring a knowledge of Elizabethan playing, and in forming some notion of what was uppermost in Shakespeare's mind when he wrote his plays, we should have had representations which, if possibly less pictorially successful, would have been more dramatic, more human, and more consistent.

To use a homely image, the question of the stage representation of Shakespeare's plays is just the question of the foot and the shoe. Must we cut off a toe here, and slice off a little from the heel there; or stretch the shoe upon the last, and, if need be, even buy a new pair of shoes? It is not enough to say that modern audiences demand "curtain" and scenery for Shakespeare's plays. No public demands what is not offered to it. Before demand can create supply, a sample of the new ware must be shown. Most modern playgoers are unaware of the methods of Elizabethan stage - playing, and therefore cannot condemn them as unsatisfactory. They may have heard something about old tapestry, rushes, and boards, but they have no reason to infer that our greatest dramatists were "thoroughly handicapped by the methods of representation then in vogue."

It is indeed to be regretted that no scholar nor actor has thought it necessary to study the art of Shakespeare's dramatic construction from the original copies. Some of our University men have written intelligently about Shakespeare's characters and his philosophy, and one of them has done something more than this. But it is doubtful if any serious attention has been given yet to the way Shakespeare conducts his story and brings his characters on and off the stage, a matter of the highest moment, since the very life of the play depends upon the skill with which this is done. And how many realize that the art of Shakespeare's dramatic construction differs fundamentally from that of the modern dramatist? In fact, a Pinero would no more know how to set about writing a play for the Elizabethan stage, in which the characters appear in the course of the story in twenty-six different localities during twenty-six years, than Shakespeare would know how to make twenty-six persons live their lives through a whole play in one room or on one day.

THE MERCHANT OF VENICE.*

The story of this play is as follows. In the opening scene, the words of Antonio to Bassanio—

> " Well, tell me now, what lady is the same
> To whom you swore a secret pilgrimage,
> That you *to-day* promised to tell me of ?"

And Lorenzo's apology for withdrawing—

> " My lord Bassanio, since you have *found* Antonio
> We two will leave you :"

and that of Salarino—

> " We'll make our leisures to attend on *yours* "—

lead us to suppose that Bassanio has come by appointment to meet Antonio, and that Antonio should be represented on his entrance as somewhat anxiously expecting his friend, and we may further presume from Solanio's words to Salarino in Act II., Scene 8—

> " I think he only loves the world for *him* "—

that there is a special cause for Antonio's sadness, beyond what he chooses to admit to his companions, and that is the knowledge that he is about to lose Bassanio's society.

With regard to Bassanio, we learn, in this first scene, that he is already indebted to Antonio, that he desires to borrow more money from his friend, to free himself from debt, before seeking the hand of Portia, a rich heiress, and that Portia has herself encouraged him to woo her.   In fact, we are at once deterred from associating purely sordid motives

* Part of a paper read before the *New Shakspere Society* in June, 1887.

with Bassanio's courtship by his glowing description of her virtues and beauty, as also by Antonio's high opinion of Bassanio's character.

Antonio, however, has not the money at hand, and it is arranged that Bassanio is to borrow the required sum on Antonio's security. The entrance of Gratiano is skilfully timed to dispel the feeling of depression that Antonio's sadness would otherwise leave upon the audience, and to give the proper comedy tone to the opening scene of a play of comedy.

In Scene 2 we are introduced to the heroine and her attendant, and learn, what probably Bassanio did not know, that Portia by her father's will is powerless to bestow her hand on the man of her choice, the stratagem, as Nerissa supposes, being devised to insure Portia's obtaining "one that shall rightly love." This we may call the first or casket-complication. Portia's strong sense of humour is revealed to us in her description of the suitors "that are already come," and her moral beauty in her determination to respect her father's wishes. " If I live to be as old as Sibylla, I will die as chaste as Diana, unless I be obtained by the manner of my father's will." The action of the play is not, however, continued till Nerissa questions Portia about Bassanio, in a passage that links this scene to the last, and confirms, in the minds of the audience, the truth of the lover's statement—

> " Sometimes from her eyes
> I did receive fair speechless messages."

A servant enters to announce the leave-taking of four of the suitors, who care not to submit to the conditions of the will, and to herald the arrival of a fifth, the Prince of Morocco.

We now come to the third scene of the play. Bassanio enters conversing with one, of whom no previous mention has been made but whose first utterance tells us he is the man of whom the required loan is demanded, and before the scene has ended, we discover further that he is to be the chief agent in bringing about the second, or pound-of-flesh-complication. There are no indications given us of Shylock's personal appearance, except that he has been dubbed "old Shylock," which is, perhaps, more an expression of contempt than of age, for he is never spoken of as old man, or old Jew, and is chiefly addressed simply as Shylock or Jew ; but the epithet is one recognized widely enough for Shylock himself to quote—

> "Well, thou shalt see, thy eyes shall be thy judge,
> The difference of *old Shylock* and Bassanio :"

as also does the Duke—

> "Antonio and *old Shylock* both stand forth."

So was it with Silas Marner. George Eliot writes : "He was so withered and yellow that though he was not yet forty the children always called him 'old master Marner.'" However, the language that Shakespeare has put into the mouth of Shylock does not impress us as being that of a man whose physical and mental faculties are in the least impaired by age ; so vigorous is it at times that Shylock might be pictured as being an Edmund Kean-like figure, with piercing black eyes and an elastic step. From Shylock's expression, "the *ancient* grudge I bear him," and Antonio's abrupt manner towards Shylock, we may conclude that the two men are avowed enemies, and have been so for some time previous to the opening of the play. This fact should, from the very first, be made evident to the audience by the emphasis Shylock gives to Antonio's name, an emphasis that is repeated every time the name occurs till he has made sure there is no doubt about who the man is that shall become bound.

The dramatic purpose of this scene is to show us Shylock directly plotting to take the life of Antonio, and the means he employs to this end are contrived with much skill. Shylock, in his opening soliloquy, discloses his intention to the audience, and at once deprives himself of its sympathy by admitting that his motives are guided more by personal considerations than by religious convictions—

> "I hate him for he is a Christian,
> But *more* for that in low simplicity
> He lends out money gratis and brings down
> The rate of usance here with us in Venice."

The three first scenes should be so acted on the stage as to accentuate in the minds of the audience (1) that Bassanio is the very dear friend of Antonio; (2) that Portia and Bassanio are in love with each other; (3) that Antonio and Shylock are avowed enemies; (4) that Shylock conspires against Antonio's life with full intent to take it should the bond become forfeit.

We are again at Belmont and witness the entrance of the Prince of Morocco, and the whole scene has a poetic dignity and repose which form a striking contrast to the preceding one. We get in the character of the Prince of Morocco a preliminary sketch of Shakespeare's Othello, and certainly the

actor, to do justice to the part, should have the
voice and presence of a Salvini. The second scene
shows us the Jew's man about to leave his rich
master to become the follower of Bassanio, and the
latter, now possessed of Shylock's money, preparing his outfit for the journey to Belmont, whither
Gratiano also is bent on going. There is, besides,
some talk of merrymaking at night-time, which fitly
leads up to our introduction to Jessica in the next
scene, and prepares us to hear of her intrigue with
Lorenzo. Jessica is the third female character in
the play, and the dramatist intends her to appear,
in contrast to Portia and Nerissa, as a tragic figure,
dark, pale, melancholy, demure, yet chaste in thought
and in action, and with a heart susceptible of tender
and devoted love. She plans her elopement with
the same fixedness of purpose as the father pursues
his revenge. In Scene 4 the elopement incident
is advanced a step by Lorenzo receiving Jessica's
directions "how to take her from her father's house,"
and a little further in the next scene, by Shylock
being got out of the way, when we hear Jessica's
final adieu. It is worth noting in this scene that,
at a moment when we are ready to sympathize with
Shylock, who is about to lose his daughter, the
dramatist denies us that privilege by further illustrating the malignancy of the man's character. He
has had an unlucky dream; he anticipates trouble
falling upon his house; he is warned by Launcelot
that there are to be masques at night; he admits
that he is not invited to Bassanio's feast out of love,
but out of flattery, and still he can say—

> " But yet I'll go *in hate*, to feed upon
> The prodigal Christian."

No personal inconvenience must hinder the acceleration of Antonio's downfall.

In Scene 6 the elopement takes place, but is almost prevented by the entrance of Antonio, whose solemn voice ringing clear on the stillness of the night is a fine dramatic contrast to the whispering of the lovers.

Shakespeare now thinks it time to return to Belmont, and we are shown the Prince of Morocco making his choice of the caskets, and we learn his fate. But he bears his disappointment like a hero, and his dignified retreat moves Portia to exclaim: "A *gentle* riddance!"

Scene 8 is one of narration only, but the speakers are in an excited frame of mind. The opening lines are intended to show that Antonio was not concerned in the flight of Jessica, and our interest in his character is further strengthened by the touching description of his farewell to Bassanio.

Scene 9 disposes of the second of Portia's remaining suitors, and, being comic in character, is inserted with good effect between two tragic scenes. The keynote to its action is to be found in Portia's words: "O, these *deliberate* fools!" The Prince of Morocco was a warrior, heroic to the tips of his fingers; the Prince of Arragon is a fop, an affected ass, a man "full of wise saws and modern instances," and the audience should be prepared for a highly amusing scene by the liveliness with which Nerissa announces his approach. His mannerism is indicated to us in such expressions as "Ha! let me see," and "Well, but to my choice." He should walk deliberately, speak deliberately, pause deliberately, and when he becomes sentimental, "pose." Highly conscious of his own superiority, and unwilling to "jump with *common* spirits" and "rank me with the *barbarous* multitudes," he assumes superiority, and gets his reward in the shape of a portrait of a blinking idiot. In fact, the whims of this Malvolio are intended to put everyone on and off the stage into high spirits, and even Portia is carried away by the fun as she mimics the retiring suitor in her exclamation to the servant. The scene ends with the announcement that Bassanio, "Lord Love," is on his way to Belmont, and we go on at once to Act III., Scene 1, which, I take it, is a continuation of Act II., Scene 8, and which, therefore, should not form part of another act.

The scene opens with Salarino and Solanio hurrying on the stage anxiously questioning each other about Antonio's rumoured loss at sea. Shylock follows almost immediately, to whom they at once turn in the hope of hearing news. It is usual on the stage to omit the entrance of Antonio's man, but apart from the dramatic effect produced by a follower of Antonio coming on to the stage at that moment, his appearance puts an end to the controversy, which otherwise would probably continue. Salarino and Solanio leave the stage awed almost to breathlessness, and Tubal enters. Then follows a piteous scene as we see Shylock's outbursts of grief, rage, and despair over the loss of his gold; yet is his anguish aggravated by the one from whom of all others he had a right to expect sympathy. But Shylock, after Tubal's words, "But Antonio is certainly undone," mutters, "Nay, that's true, that's very true," and takes from his purse a coin, and with a countenance and gesture expressive of indomitable purpose, continues : "*Go*, Tubal, fee me an officer; bespeak him a *fortnight* before. I will have the *heart* of him if he forfeit. . . . *Go*, Tubal, and meet me at our synagogue. *Go*, good Tubal; at our synagogue, Tubal."

Shylock's misfortunes in this scene would arouse sympathy were it not for the damning confession to Tubal of his motive for hating Antonio "for were he out of Venice I can make what merchandise I will." Words that Jessica's lines prove are not idle ones.

> "When I was with him I have heard him swear
>   To Tubal and to Chus, his countrymen,
>   That he would rather have Antonio's flesh
>   Than twenty times the value of the sum
>   That he did owe him."

Act III., Scene 2, brings us to the last stage of the casket complication, and here Shakespeare, to avoid sameness, directs that a song shall be sung while Bassanio is occupied in deciding his fate; so that his long speech is spoken after the choice has been made, the leaden casket being then in his hands, and his words merely used to justify his decision. That Bassanio must win Portia is realized from the first. Moreover, his success, after Shylock's threats in the last scene, has become a dramatic necessity, and is thus saved from an appearance of unreality, so that his love adventure develops naturally. His good fortune is Gratiano's; then news is brought of Antonio's bankruptcy and Bassanio is sent to his friend's relief. Scene 3 does no more than show in action what was previously narrated by Solanio in the preceding one,

for the Elizabethan dramatists, differing in their
methods from the Greeks, rarely allowed narration
to take the place of action on the stage. Perhaps
this was on account of the mixed character of
the audience, the "groundlings" being too busy
cracking nuts to take in an important situation
merely from its narration. To them Antonio's
danger would not become a fact till they actually
saw the man in irons and the jailor by his side.
In the fourth scene we go back to Belmont to hear
that Portia and Nerissa are to be present at the
trial, though with what object we are not told. We
hear, also, of Portia's admiration for Antonio, whose
character she compares with that of her husband.
Scene 5 being comic, well serves its purpose as a
contrast to the tragic intensity displayed in the
scene which follows. Here, too, Portia and Bassanio
win golden opinions from Jessica :

> "It is very meet,
> The Lord Bassanio live an upright life ;
>   For having such a blessing in his lady,
> He finds the joys of heaven here on earth ; . . .
>   Why, if two gods should play some heavenly match,
> And on the wager lay two earthly women,
>   And Portia one, there must be something else
> Pawn'd with the other, for the poor rude world
>   Hath not her fellow."

The trial scene is so well known that I shall not
dwell upon it except to mention that I think the
dramatist intended the scene to be acted with
more vigour and earnestness on the part of
all the characters than is represented on the
modern stage, and with more vehemence on the
part of Shylock. Conscious of his lawful right,

he defies the duke and council in language not at all respectful,

> "What if my house be troubled with a rat,
>   And I be pleased to give *ten* thousand ducats
> To have it baned ?"

When Shylock is worsted the traditional business is for him to leave the stage with the air of a martyr going to his execution, and thus produce a tragic climax where none is wanted. We seem to get an indication of what should be Shylock's behaviour in his hour of adversity by reading the Italian version of the story, with which Shakespeare was familiar. "Everyone present was greatly pleased and deriding the Jew said: ' He who laid traps for others, is caught himself.' The Jew seeing he could gain nothing, tore in pieces the bond *in a great rage.*" Indeed, Shylock's words,

> "Why, then the devil give him good of it !
> I'll stay no longer question,"

are exactly suited to the action of tearing up the bond. Certain it is that only by Shylock being "in a great rage," as he rushes off the stage, can the audience be greatly pleased, and in a fit humour to be interested in the further doings of Portia. Scene 2 of this act is generally omitted on the stage, though it seems to me necessary in order to show how Nerissa gets possession of Gratiano's ring; it also affords an opportunity for some excellent business on the part of Nerissa, who walks off arm in arm with her husband, unknown to him.

The last act is the shortest fifth act in the Globe edition, and if deficient in action Shakespeare gives it another interest by the wealth and music of its poetry, a device more than once made use of by him to strengthen undramatic material. Shakespeare's knowledge of the value of sound, in dramatic effect, is shown by Launcelot interrupting the whispering of the lovers, and profaning the stillness of the night with his halloas, which have a similar effect to the nurse's calls in the balcony scene of Romeo and Juliet; it is also shown by the music, and in the tucket sound; while the picture brought to the imagination, by allusion to the light burning in Portia's hall, gives reality to the scene.

ROMEO AND JULIET.*

The argument that Arthur Brooke affixes to his poem, "Romeus and Iuliet," runs as follows:

> "Loue hath inflamed twayne by sodayn sight,
> And both do graunt the thing that both desyre :
> They wed in shrift, by counsell of a frier.
> Yong Romeus clymes fayre Iuliets bower by night,
> Three monthes he doth enjoy his cheefe delight.
> By Tybalts rage, prouoked unto yre,
> He payeth death to Tybalt for his hyre.
> A banisht man, he scapes by secret flight,
> New mariage is offred to his wyfe.
> She drinkes a drinke that seemes to reue her breath,
> They bury her, that sleping yet hath lyfe.
> Her husband heares the tydinges of her death :
> He drinkes his bane. And she with Romeus knyfe,
> When she awakes, her selfe (alas) she sleath."

And the title of the same story in William Painter's "Palace of Pleasure," is on the same lines:

> "The goodly Hystory of the true, and constant Loue betweene Rhomeo and Iulietta, the one of whom died of Poyson, and the

---

* Read at the meeting of the *New Shakspere Society*, Friday, April 12, 1889.

other of sorrow, and heuinesse : wherein be comprysed many aduentures of Loue, and other deuises touchinge the same."

Here is Shakespeare's Prologue to his adaptation of the story for the stage :

> " Two housholds, both alike in dignitie,
> In faire Verona, where we lay our Scene,
> From auncient grude breake to new mutinie
> Where ciuill bloud makes ciuill hands uncleane.
> From forth the fatall loynes of these two foes
> A paire of starre-crost louers take their life ;
> Whose misaduentur'd pittious overthrowes
> Doth, with their death, burie their Parents strife.
> The fearfull passage of their death-markt loue,
> And the continuance of their Parents rage,
> Which, but their childrens end, nought could remoue,
> Is now the two houres trafficque of our Stage ;
> The which, if you with patient eares attend,
> What here shall misse, our toyle shall striue to mend."

Why the dramatist thought fit to choose a different motive for his tragedy to the one shown in the poem and the novel, we shall never know. He may have found the hatred of the two houses accentuated in an older play on this subject, and his unerring dramatic instinct would prompt him to use the parents' strife as a lurid background on which to portray with greater vividness the "fearfull passage" of the "starre-crost louers"; or the modification may have been due to his reflections upon the political and religious strife of his day; or to his irritation at Brooke's short-sightedness in upholding, as more deserving of censure, the passion of im- provident love than the evil of ready-made hatred. Whatever be the reason, the fact remains that Shake- speare, who was not partial to Prologues, has in this instance made use of one to indicate the lines that guide the action of his play, and it is upon these lines that I propose to-night to discuss the stage representation.

I divide the characters into three groups. Those who belong to the House of Capulet, the House of Montague, and those who, as partisans of neither of the houses, we may call the neutrals. These include Escalus, Mercutio, Paris, Friar Laurence, Friar John, an apothecary, and all the citizens of any position and standing, the Italian municipalities being ever anxious to repress the feuds of nobles.

The play opens with a renewal of hostilities between the two houses, which serves not only as a striking opening, but brings on to the stage many of the chief actors without unnecessary delay. In less than thirty lines we are introduced to seven persons, all of whom indicate their character by the attitude they assume towards the quarrel. We are shown the peace-loving Benvolio, the fiery Tybalt, the imperious and vigorous Capulet, calling for his two-handed sword—

"What noyse is this? giue me my long sword, hoe !"—

his characterless wife, feebly echoing her husband's moodiness—

" A crowch, a crowch, why call you for a sword ?"

and the calm dignity of Romeo's mother—

" Thou shalt not stir one foote to seeke a foe."

We are also shown the citizens hastily arming themselves to part the two houses, and hear for the first time their ominous shout :

" Downe with the Capulets, downe with the Mountagues."

It is heard on two subsequent occasions during the play, and is the death-knell of the lovers. The quarrel is abruptly terminated by the entrance of the Prince, who speaks with a precision and decision which throws every other character on the stage into insignificance, and stamps him at once in our eyes as a central figure. After the belligerents disperse, admonished by the Prince that death awaits the next offender against the peace, a scene follows to prepare us for Romeo's entrance, Shakespeare having wisely kept him out of the quarrel, that the audience may see him indifferent to every other passion but the one of love. Romeo, until he had been shot with Cupid's arrow, seems to have passed for a pleasant companion, as we learn from Mercutio's words, spoken to him in the third act :

"Why is not this better now, than groning for loue ; now art thou sociable, now art thou Romeo : now art thou what thou art, by art as well as by nature."

Romeo's romantic temperament naturally leads him into a love affair of a sufficiently compromising character to need being kept from the knowledge of his parents. Brooke narrates Rosaline's reception of Romeo's passion :

"But she that from her youth was fostred euermore,
     With vertues foode, and taught in schole of wisdomes
         skillful lore :
     By aunswere did cutte of th' affections of his loue,
     That he no more occasion had so vayne a sute to moue."

And Shakespeare gives to Romeo almost similar words :

"And in strong proofe of chastitie well armd,
     From loues weak childish bow she liues uncharmd ;
     Shee will not stay the siege of louing tearmes,
     Nor bide th' incounter of assailing eies,
     Nor ope her lap to sainct seducing gold."

A note in the Irving stage-version, referring to Mercutio's words, "stabd with a white wenches blacke eye," states that "a pale woman with black eyes" is suggestive of a wanton nature. Is this Rosaline's character? If we are to accept seriously Mercutio's words as being the poet's description of Rosaline's personal appearance, we may also give a literal interpretation to the following lines:

> " I conjure thee by Rosaline's bright eyes,
> By her high forehead, and her Scarlet lip."

In Charlotte Brontë's opinion, a high forehead was an indication of conscientiousness; she could get on, she would say, with anyone "who had a lump at the top of the head." The reproaches of the Friar are, in my opinion, levelled against Romeo, and not Rosaline. Romeo says:

> " Thou chidst me oft for louing Rosaline."

And the Friar replies:

> " For doting, not for louing, pupill mine."

Romeo could not openly woo one who was of the House of Capulet, and Rosaline would not tolerate a clandestine courtship.

In Scene 2 allusion is made for the second time to the quarrel of the two houses. We also hear of Juliet for the first time, and are shown Paris, no less a person than the Prince's kinsman, as a suitor for her hand. The assumed dignity and good breeding of Capulet in this scene are to be noted. The Irving acting-version leaves out the whole of the servant's very amusing speech about the shoemaker and his "yard." Why are virtuous tragedians always anxious to rob the low comedians of their cakes and ale ?

In Scene 3 we are introduced to our principal comic character, the Nurse, brought into the play no doubt to supply "those unsavoury morsels of unseemly sentences, which doth so content the hungry humours of the rude multitude." We are shown Juliet, and hear again of Paris, whose high rank and fine clothes have won the simple mother's heart, but Juliet's independence of character is indicated in the line :

> " Ile looke to like, if looking liking moue."

And a touch of subtlety is revealed to us in the words :

> " But no more deepe will I endart mine eye,
> Than your consent giues strength to make (it) flie."

In Scene 4 Mercutio is brought on to the stage ; a character that figures in many Elizabethan plays, and in the theatrical parlance of the poet's time was known as the "braggart" soldier, and yet the part had never received such brilliant treatment till Shakespeare took it in hand. Scene 5 is the hall in Capulet's house, where Romeo and Juliet see each other for the first time, the audience now being fully aware of the conditions under which the two meet. It has seen the hatred of the houses; the purse-proud Capulet contracting a fashionable marriage for his daughter; Romeo's melancholy ; his longing for the love and sympathy of woman ; and Juliet's loneliness amid conventional and uncongenial sur-roundings. The sight of a Montague within

Capulet's house gives warning for a fresh outbreak
of hostilities—

> "but this intrusion shall,
> Now seeming sweet, conuert to bittrest gall"—

and Romeo's cry,

> "Is *she* a Capulet?
> O deare account! my life is my foes debt"—

and Juliet's exclamation,

> "Prodigious birth of loue it is to mee,
> That I must loue a loathed *enemie!*"

foreshadow the doom prophesied by Romeo as about
to begin "with this night's reuels."

In the rebuke of Tybalt we get an indication of
Capulet's character. A note in the Irving-version
states that Capulet is a meddlesome mollycoddle
not unlike Polonius. But the fussiness of Polonius
proceeds from his vanity, from his mental and
physical impotence. Capulet's activity is the outcome of a love for domineering that springs from
his pride of birth, and his consciousness of physical
superiority. Tybalt, who is no child, sinks into
insignificance at the thunder of this man's voice:

> "He shall be endured.
> What goodman boy, I say he shall, go too.
> Am I the master here, or you? go too,
> Youle not endure him, god shall mend my soule, . . .
> You will set cock a hoope, youle be the man . . .
> You must contrarie *me.*"

Capulet, I fear, would have annihilated the bloodless
and decorous Polonius with the breath of his nostrils.
Women who marry men of this overbearing character
often lose their own individuality, and become mere

ciphers. So does Lady Capulet. She dare not call her soul her own; she cannot be mistress even in the kitchen. It is Capulet's indignation at his nephew's interference with his affairs that prepares us for his outburst of passion, in the fourth act, when his daughter threatens opposition to his will.

At the close of Scene 5 Shakespeare thinks it necessary to bring the Chorus on to the stage in order to make known to the audience the direction in which the future action of the play will turn, and to account for the suppression of Rosaline, of whom, until the entrance of Juliet, so much has been said. That the words were not printed in the first quarto, a piratical version published from notes taken at a performance of the play, seems to suggest that after the first representation the Chorus did not appear on the stage, for the speech was found to be an unnecessary interruption.

Presuming, therefore, that there is no delay in the progress of the action, Romeo returns from the ball, and, giving his companions the slip, hides himself in Capulet's orchard, where he hears their taunts about his Rosaline. The value, to the poet, of the Rosaline episode is thus further shown by the use he makes of it to conceal from Romeo's inquisitive companions this second love intrigue, so fraught with danger. That David Garrick, in his acting-version, should allow Mercutio to make open fun of Romeo's love for the daughter and heiress of old Capulet proves how rarely the actor is able to replace the author.

It is incomprehensible to me why our stage Juliets, in the "Balcony Scene," go through their billing-and-cooing as deliberately as they do their toilets, never for a moment thinking that the "place is death" to

Romeo, and that "loves sweet bait must be stolen from fearful hookes." In Shakespeare's time this scene was acted in broad daylight, and the dramatist is careful to stimulate the imagination of his audience with appropriate imagery. The word "night" occurs ten times, and I suppose the actor would be instructed to give a special emphasis to it. There are, besides, several allusions to the moon and the stars, including that descriptive couplet:

> " Lady, by yonder blessed Moone I vow,
> That tips with siluer all these frute tree tops."

When Shakespeare could give us in words so vivid a picture of moonlight, Ben Jonson could well afford to have a fling at Inigo Jones's mechanical scenery, and say:

> " What poesy e'er was painted on a wall?"

Romeo goes direct from Capulet's orchard to Friar Lawrence's cell to make confession of his " deare hap." He loves now in earnest, and love teaches him to brave all dangers, and even to face matrimony; and his virtuous mood wins for him the good-will of the Friar, who sees in the alliance of the two houses their reconciliation. In the poem and novel both the lovers avow a similar disinterested motive to justify their union, but the mind of reason never enters the heart of love, and Shakespeare, in their case, wisely omits this bit of sophistry. The advance of the love episode must move side by side with the quarrel episode, so in the next scene we hear of Romeo receiving a challenge from Tybalt. The Irving-version omits most of the good-natured banter between Romeo and Mercutio, which is all telling comedy if spoken lightly and quickly. The

Nurse enters, and Mercutio and Benvolio set off for Montague's house, where they propose dining. The incident that follows must have been very irritating to the Elizabethan Puritans, who complained of the corruption of morals begot in " the chapel of Satan " by witnessing the carrying and recarrying of letters by laundresses " to beguile fathers of their children." Here more excellent comedy is omitted in the Irving-version, including the Nurse's allusion to Paris as being " the properer man " of the two, and her naïve question, " Doth not Rosemarie and Romeo begin both with a letter ?" The Nurse had overheard Juliet talk about "Rosemarie and Romeo." Later on we see rosemary strewed over the body of the apparently dead Juliet.

The scene in which Romeo and Juliet meet to be married at the Friar's Cell ends on the stage the second act. But to drop the curtain here interrupts the dramatic movement just as it is about to reach a climax in the death of Tybalt, followed by the banishment of Romeo. These incidents require action that is all hurry and excitement, and are therefore out of place at the beginning of an act, unless it be the opening act of a play. Besides, they are immediately connected with the scene in which allusion is made to Tybalt having challenged Romeo. We are shown Mercutio and Benvolio returning from Montague's house, where they proposed dining. And Mercutio has, apparently, indulged too freely in his host's wine, for the prudent Benvolio is anxious to get his friend out of the public streets as quickly as possible. Benvolio's worst fears are realized by the entrance of the quarrelsome Tybalt, whom Mercutio, as is the way with fuddled people, at once offers to fight. But Tybalt hesitates to cross swords with a relative of the Prince, and is glad of the excuse of Romeo's appearance to transfer the quarrel to him. Romeo will not draw sword upon his wife's cousin, and Mercutio, exasperated, takes up the challenge, is stabbed by Tybalt under Romeo's arm, and dies cursing the two houses. This tragedy rouses Romeo to action; he will now defend his own honour since he was Mercutio's dear friend. Tybalt is challenged and killed. The citizens "are up," and for the second time we hear their ominous shout :

"Downe with the Capulets, downe with the Montagues !"

They enter, followed by the Prince, with the heads of the two houses and their wives. The Capulets call for Romeo's death. The Montagues protest that Romeo in killing a man whose life was already forfeited has but taken the law into his own hands. For that offence he is exiled by the Prince.

"I haue an interest in your hates proceeding :
    My bloud for your rude brawles doth lie a bleeding.
    But ile amerce you with so strong a fine,
    That you shall all repent the losse of mine.
    I will be deafe to pleading and excuses,
    Nor teares, nor prayers, shall purchase out abuses.
    Therefore use none, let Romeo hence in hast,
    Else when he is found, that houre is his last."

The whole of the latter part of this scene is brilliant in the variety and rapidity of its action, and should not, I consider, be omitted in representation as is directed to be done in the Irving-version. To take out the second renewal of hostilities between the two houses; not to show, in action on the stage, the rage of the Capulets at the death of

Tybalt, and the grief of the Montagues at the banishment of Romeo, is to weaken the tragic significance of the scenes that follow. Without it the audience cannot vividly realize that the hatred of the two houses has reached its acutest stage, and that all hope of reconciliation is at an end.

Mercutio at the commencement of this scene says to Benvolio: " Thou wilt quarell with a man for cracking nuts, having no other reason but because thou hast hazel eyes." Did Shakespeare, who, according to tradition had hazel eyes, act the part of Benvolio ? I think he did. It is the only part in the play I can fancy him able to act. A study of both the bust and the Droeshout portrait of the poet-dramatist leads me to believe that he would not have been able to disguise easily his identity on the stage. His flexibility was essentially of a mental and not of a physical nature. The face is entirely wanting in mobility, and the head is so large that no wig could hide its unusual size. Shakespeare, moreover, became bald probably early in life. The Droeshout portrait shows undoubtedly the likeness of a youngish man, about thirty-five years old, while his baldness would still justify the epithet of " grandsire " with which Mercutio dubs Benvolio ; and " grandsire " may have been a nickname of Shakespeare's suggested by his baldness. " Come hither, goodman baldpate "—words spoken by Lucio in " Measure for Measure " — have been quoted as a reason for presuming that Shakespeare played the Duke in that comedy. Sir William Davenant, who liked to be thought a natural son of the poet, in an adaption of this play altered the words to, " She has been advised by a bald dramatic poet of the next cloister." If the audience recognized their "gentle Will" in the part of the peace-loving Benvolio, we may imagine the laughter that would arise at Mercutio's words : "Thy head is as full of quarelles, as an egg is full of meate"—Shakespeare's head being egg-shaped. If my supposition be correct, we may honour the self-abnegation, the entire absence of personal vanity that enabled Shakespeare, like Molière, to direct laughter against himself. The scattered references to him which we find in the writings of his contemporaries show us, says Professor Dowden, "the poet concealed and some-times forgotten in the man, and make it clear that he moved among his fellows with no assuming of the bard or prophet, no air of authority as of one divinely commissioned ; that, on the contrary, he appeared as a pleasant comrade, genial, gentle, full of civility in the large meaning of the word, upright in dealing, ready and bright in wit, quick and sportive in conversation." How aptly does this description fit the character of Benvolio ! One quality was especially common to the two men— tact. It was the possession of tact that made Shakespeare so invaluable to his fellow - actors as a manager. Benvolio's tact is shown in his conversation with Romeo's parents, with Romeo himself, with Mercutio when hot-headed, and with the Prince, Mercutio's relative. It is true that Benvolio attributes Mercutio's death to Tybalt's interference, while in reality it was due to Mer-cutio's indiscretion ; but we have no pity for Tybalt, who, as Brooke says, thirsting after the death of others, lost his life.

Romeo's banishment brings us to the middle and "busy" part of the play, where the Elizabethan actors were expected to thunder their loudest to split the ears of the groundlings; and Shakespeare, not yet sufficiently independent as a dramatist to dispense with the conventions of his stage, follows suit on the same fiddle to the same tune; and after all the ranting eloquence on the part of Romeo and Juliet, we are just where we were before with regard to any advance made with the story. Act III., Scene 2, is often entirely omitted in representation, but the Irving-version retains most of it. It is not till the middle of Act III., Scene 3, that the action advances again. But this, and the previous scenes, if acted with animation and rapidly spoken by all the characters concerned, would not take up much time, and could be declaimed with effect. The stage fashion of making the Friar stolidly indifferent to the unexpected complication that has arisen through Tybalt's death is not only undramatic, but inconsistent with the text. A heavy responsibility lies on him, and his position is full of difficulty and danger. The scene that follows shows us Capulet fixing a day for the marriage of Juliet with Paris, and the father's words—

> " I thinke she will be rulde
> In all respects by *me :* nay, more, I doubt it not,"

have a significance, and render the parting of the lovers in the next scene highly dramatic. In the poem and novel, Juliet, before parting with Romeo, proposes to accompany him disguised as his servant; about the best thing she could do. After a good deal of arguing on both sides the idea is abandoned

as impracticable. Shakespeare prefers his lovers to
discourse about the nightingale. Romeo being gone,
the mother enters to announce to the wife her
betrothal to Paris, and the early day of marriage.
The news is sprung upon her with terrible abrupt-
ness, though the audience have been in the secret
from the first, and Juliet has hardly time to protest
against "this sudden day of joy" before the father
enters to complete her discomfiture by his torrents
of abuse. Capulet's varnish of good manners entirely
disappears in this scene, and his coarse nature
is exposed in all its ugliness. But in the emer-
gency of this tragic moment, as Professor Dowden
points out, does Juliet leap into womanhood, and
realize her position and responsibilities as a wife,
and in the following lines Shakespeare touches the
first note of highest tragedy in the play : that of the
mind's suffering as opposed to the mere tragedy of
incident—

> "O God, ô Nurse, how shall this be preuented ?
> My husband is on earth, my faith in heauen ;
> How shall that faith returne againe to earth,
> Unlesse that husband send it me from heauen
> By leauing earth ? comfort me, counsaile me."

I am curious to learn on what grounds these thrilling words are omitted in the Irving-version. To
me they are the climax of the scene and of the play
so far as it has progressed. They mark the turning-
point in Juliet's moral nature. They enable us to
forgive her any indiscretions of which she may previously have been guilty. From this point onwards
all is calm in Juliet's breast, because there is no
infirmity of purpose,

> "If all else faile, my self have power to die."

As the shadows fall across the path of the lovers, so do they over that of the Friar.

> " O *Iuliet*, I already know thy greefe,
>   It straines me past the compasse of my wits,"

is his greeting in the next scene. A " desperate preventive " to shame or death is decided upon, and then follows what is perhaps the most dramatic episode in the whole play. We are shown Capulet's household busy with the preparations for the marriage-feast, and the father, now bent on having a " great ado," hastily summoning " twenty cunning Cookes " — the consequence possibly of Juliet's threatened opposition to his wishes. Juliet enters to feign submission and beg forgiveness, which enables the father to indulge in another despotic freak by hastening the day of marriage, heedless of all the inconvenience it may cause. Juliet retires to her chamber, and Capulet goes to prepare Paris against to-morrow. Then comes Juliet's terrible ordeal, the undertaking " of a thing like death," which is all the more terrible because it must be done alone. This scene is often overacted on the stage. Our Juliets do far too much " stumping and frumping " about. I once saw the " potion-scene " acted with dramatic intelligence by an actress quite unknown to fame. When Juliet lays her dagger on the table, the actress took up the vial, and, standing motionless in the centre of the stage, spoke the lines in a hurried, low whisper, conveying the impression of reflection as well as the need for discretion. At the words,

> " O looke, me thinks I see my Cozins Ghost,"

she sank on one knee, and, raising the right arm
with a quick movement, pointed into space, the eye
following the hand, a very simple but telling gesture.
The words, "Stay, *Tybalt*, stay!" were not given
with a scream, but in a tone of alarm and entreaty,
followed immediately by the drinking of the potion,
as if to suggest Juliet's desire to come to Romeo's
rescue. The whole scene was acted in less than
two minutes. The vision of Tybalt's ghost pursuing
Romeo for vengeance, an incident not to be found
in the originals, shows the touch of the master
dramatist. We feel the need of some immediate in-
centive to nerve Juliet to raise the vial to her lips;
and what more effectual than that of her overwrought
imagination picturing to herself the husband in
danger.

While the poor child lies prostrate upon her bed
in the likeness of death, we are shown the dawn of
the morning, the rousing and bustle of the household; we hear the bridal march in the distance, the
sound coming nearer every moment; the Nurse
knocking at Juliet's chamber-door; her awful discovery; the entrance of the parents; the filling of
the stage by the bridal party, led by the Friar; the
wailing, and wringing of the hands as the first
quarto directs; the changing of the sound of instru-
ments to that of melancholy bells, of solemn hymns
to sullen dirges, of bridal flowers to funeral wreaths.
All this is thrilling in conception, and yet the episode
as conceived by Shakespeare is never represented
on the stage. Why are the Capulet scenes omitted,
those which are dovetailed to the "potion scene,"
and make it by contrast so terribly tragic? The
accentuation here of Capulet's tyranny, of his

sensuality, his brutal frankness, his indifference to every one's convenience but his own, his delight in exacting a cringing obedience from all about him, are designed by the dramatist to move us with deep pity for Juliet's sufferings, and by emphasizing its necessity to save the "potion scene" from the danger of appearing grotesque. But Shakespeare's method of dramatic composition, that of uniting a series of short scenes with each other in one dramatic movement, will not bear the elaboration of heavy stage sets, and with the demand for carpentry comes the inducement for mutilation. At the Shakespeare Reading Society's recital of this play, given recently under my direction at the London Institution, these scenes were spoken without delay or interruption, and with but one scene announced, and the interest and breathless attention they aroused among the audience convinced me that my conception as to the dramatic treatment of them was the right one. Until these scenes are restored to the acting version, Shakespeare's tragedy will not be seen on the stage as he conceived it; and when they are restored, their dramatic power will electrify the house, and twentieth-century dilettantism will lose its influence among playgoers. The comic scene between Peter and the Musicians should also be restored. It comes in as a welcome relief after the intensity of the previous scenes, and is, besides, a connecting link with the comedy in the earlier part of the play.

The last act can be briefly dealt with. We anticipate the final catastrophe, though we do not know by what means it will be brought about. It is carried out, as it should be, effectively but simply.

The children have loved and suffered, let them die easily and quickly. Romeo's costume in exile is described in the poem as that of a merchant venturer, which is certainly a more appropriate dress than the conventional black velvet of the stage. After hearing the fatal news, which provokes the boy to mutter, " Is it even so ?" in the Lyceum version is inserted the stage-direction, " *He pauses, overcome with grief.*" But as there is no similar stage-direction in the originals, the actor may, without violation to the author's intentions, pause *before* the words are spoken. The blow is too sudden, too cruel, too overwhelming to allow of any immediate response in words. The colour would fly from Romeo's face, his teeth grip his under lip, his eyes gleam with a look of frenzy, *looks* that " import some misadventure," but there is no action and no sound for a while, and afterwards only a muttering. The stillness of Romeo's desperation is very dramatic. There is nothing, in my opinion, unnatural in Romeo's description of the Apothecary's shop. All sorts of petty details float before our mental vision when the nerves are over-wrought, but the actor should be careful not to accentuate the description in any way ; it is but introductory to the dominant words of the speech,

" And if a man did need a poyson now."

As Juliet's openly acknowledged lover, Paris occupies too prominent a place in the play to be lightly dismissed, and so he is involved in the final catastrophe. In Brooke's poem, Romeo, before dying, prays to Heaven for mercy and forgiveness, and the picture of the boy kneeling by his wife's

side, with her hand clasped in his, pleading to his
Redeemer to—

"Take pity on my sinnefull and my poore afflicted mynde!"

would, on the stage, have been a supremely pathetic
situation. But Shakespeare's stern love of dramatic
truth rejects it. In Romeo's character he strikes
but one note, love—and love as a passion. Love is
Romeo's divinity, physical beauty his deity. The
assertion that—

> " In nature there's no blemish but the mind,
> None can be call'd deform'd but the unkind,"

would have sounded in Romeo's ears profanation.
When he first sees Juliet he will by touching hers
make *blessed* his rude hand, and when he dies he will
seal the doors of breath "with a *righteous* kiss." To
the Friar he cries :

> " Do thou but close our hands with holy words,
> Then loue-deuouring death do what he dare.
> It is inough I may but call her *mine*."

And "love-devouring death" accepts the challenge,
but the agony of death does not "countervail the
exchange of joy" that one short minute gives him in
her presence. Here Shakespeares's treatment of the
love-episode differs from that of Brooke's in his
tolerance for the children's love, though it be carried
out in defiance of the parents' wishes, and in his
recognition that love, so long as it be strong as death,
has an ennobling and not a debasing influence on
character : we are made to feel that it is better for
Romeo to have loved and lost than never to have
loved at all. For the hatred of the two houses

Shakespeare shows no tolerance. Juliet's death is carried out with the greatest simplicity, and within a few moments of her awakening. There is neither time for reflection nor lamentation; the watch has been roused, and is heard approaching. She has hardly kissed the poison from her dead husband's lips before they enter the churchyard, and nothing but the darkness of the night screens from them the sight of the steel that Juliet plunges into her breast. It is the presence of the watch, almost within touch of her, that goads her to lift the knife, just as it is the vision of Tybalt's ghost pursuing Romeo that nerves her to drink the potion. The dramatist's intention is clearly indicated in the stage-directions of the two quartos and the folio, but the Irving-version retains in this last scene the modern stage-directions.

Professor Dowden is of opinion "that it were presumptuous to say that had Shakespeare been acquainted with the earlier form of the story (in which Juliet wakes before Romeo dies), he would not have altered his ending." But an ending of this kind is inartistic. It is bringing the axe down twice instead of once. It is introducing a new complication and a new movement at a moment when none is wanted. The catastrophe should be and always is, by Shakespeare, carried out with simplicity and directness. After Juliet's death other watchmen enter with the Friar in custody, while from afar we hear for the third and last time the cries of the citizens:

"Downe with the Capulets, downe with the Mountagues!"

the only child of each of the two rival houses lying dead before the spectators. Nature had done her best to effect a reconciliation, but man thwarted her in her purpose. Then the Prince and the heads of the two houses enter and learn for the first time that

> " *Romeo* there dead, was husband to that *Iuliet*,
> And she there dead, that's *Romeo's* faithfull wife."

Well may the Prince say—

> " *Capulet, Montague,*
> See what a scourge is laide upon your hate
> That heauen finds means to kill your joyes with loue."

All this last scene is full of animation, and presents a fine opportunity for the *régisseur.* I am obliged to use the French word, for we have no similar functionary in this country. Our public is sufficiently indifferent to the welfare of dramatic art to allow its leading actors to be their own stage-managers and often their own authors. As a consequence the public gets no English plays worthy of being called plays, and no guarantee that a dead author's intentions shall be respected. Human nature has its prejudices, and the actor is seldom to be found who can look at a play from any other point of view than in relation to the prominence of his own part in it. It is owing to the despotism of the actor on the English stage, and consequently to the star system, that I attribute the mutilation of Shakespeare's plays in their representation. The closing scene of this play might be made very effective in action. The crowd hurrying with " bated breath " to the spot; its horror at the sight of the dead children, who for all it knows are murdered; its amazement at finding they are man and wife; the Prince's stern rebuke; the bowed grief and shame of Montague and Capulet; the reconciliation of the bereaved parents, and joining of hands across the dead bodies. The Irving-version omits all but the entrance of the citizens with Montague, Capulet, and the Prince, who at once ends the play with the couplet—

> " For neuer was a Storie of more wo
> Than this of *Iuliet* and her *Romeo.*"

But if the Prince hears no story, he and those who enter with him cannot be aware that Romeo and Juliet are man and wife, or that they died by their own hands, and are not victims to an act of treachery. Then why open your play with the quarrel of the two houses if you do not intend to show them reconciled ? Why not follow the Cumberland acting-version, and take out the crowd scenes altogether ? It is a more intelligible proceeding than this compromise of the Irving-version.

Criticized as classical tragedy, the play of " Romeo and Juliet " is a veritable hotch-potch. It seems to defy the laws of criticism. The characters at one moment talk in the highest poetical language, and at another in the most commonplace colloquy. Nothing can well seem more inconsistent than to put into the mouth of Capulet these words—

> " Death lies on her like an untimely frost,
> Upon the sweetest flower of all the field."

Bombast goes side by side with poetry ; passion with pantomime. Yet, as Lessing says, " Plays which do not observe the classical rules, must yet observe rules of some kind if they are to please ;" and Shakespeare sought to establish rules in accordance with the national taste, his first aim being the combination of the serious and the ludicrous. Vigorous characterization, a vital and varied move-

ment, and the skilful handling of scenes well calculated to stir the emotions of an audience, make
"Romeo and Juliet" an acting play of enduring
interest.

In conclusion, I hold that no stage-version of
"Romeo and Juliet" is consistent with Shakespeare's intentions which does not give prominence
to the hatred of the two houses and retain intact
the three "crowd scenes"—the one at the opening of
the play, the second in the middle, and the third at
the end. To represent only the love episode is to
make that episode far less tragic, and therefore less
dramatic.

"HAMLET."*

In comparing the acting-edition of "Hamlet" with
the authorized text of the Globe edition, I find that
it is shorter by 1,191 lines, and omits the characters
of Voltemand, Cornelius, Reynaldo, a gentleman, and
Fortinbras. Such a modification should, perhaps,
exclude the acting-editions from being classed as the
same play with either the folio or second quarto. It
is a question whether 1,200 lines can be taken out of
any Shakespearian play without defeating the poet's
dramatic intentions; but if it is necessary to shorten
a play to this extent in order to make it suitable for
the stage, so important an alteration should not,
surely, be left entirely to the discretion of the actor,
but should be the work of Shakespearian scholars,
assisted by the advice of the dramatic profession.
One would think that Shakespeare's world-famed
greatness as a dramatist should make all his plays

* Read before the *New Shakspere Society*, June 10, 1881 ; published in the *Era*, July 2, 1881.

so valued by his countrymen that any alteration in their stage representation which had not been sanctioned by the highest authorities would be repudiated. But, unfortunately, it is not so. That the omission of some of the characters in the acting-edition of "Hamlet" has not impaired Shakespeare's dramatic conception of the play is at least a matter of doubt. In the second quarto we have a play constructed for the purpose of showing us types of character contrasted one with the other. Strong men, weak men, old men, fond women, all living and moving under the influence of a destiny that is not of their own seeking. We have also a Danish court in which a terrible crime has been committed, and over which an avenging angel is hovering with drawn sword waiting to descend on the head of the guilty one; and, because the influence of good in this court is too weak to conquer the evil, the sword falls on the good as well as on the evil, on the weak as well as on the strong. Something is rotten in the State of Denmark; no one there is worthy to rule; the kingdom must be taken away and given to a stranger. It is the play as an epitome of life which is interesting the mind of Shakespeare, and not the career of one individual, even though the whole play be influenced by the actions of that individual. Look at the first quarto and we find a proof of this. Mutilated as that version is, care has been taken to avoid confusing the story of the play. Everything relating to Fortinbras is kept in the quarto, because Fortinbras has to appear like Richmond in "Richard III.," as the hero who will restore peace and order to the distracted kingdom. This much-abused quarto has 557 lines less than the modern acting edition, of which 254 are not in that edition, although they are in the second quarto (or rather have a meaning equivalent to lines in the second quarto), showing clearly that it is possible to shorten the text in more ways than one. The first quarto comes nearer to Shakespeare's dramatic conception of the play than the modern stage version, because the latter, by omitting some of the persons represented, and also many of the lines which reveal the weaker side of Hamlet's character, have altered the story of the play, and placed the part of Hamlet in a different aspect to the one conceived by the author.

I will now compare French's acting-edition of "Hamlet," scene by scene, with the Globe edition. The Globe edition contains all the lines of the second quarto and the folio. It adheres to the text, but not to the stage-directions. For reading purposes, perhaps, the alterations which have been made in the latter may be justified to some extent as a necessity, yet for the acting-edition it would have been better to copy the originals. There are alterations made to the stage-directions in the first scene. Horatio, Marcellus, and the Ghost are shown to enter a line later in the Globe edition than is marked in the quarto or folio. But the attention of an audience is better sustained if the entrances of characters, especially of the Ghost, is not anticipated, and also if the dialogue is not interrupted by pauses for entrances and exits.

In comparing the text, I find that lines 69 to 125 of the Globe edition are omitted in the acting-edition. But these lines explain to the audience why Marcellus, Bernardo, and Horatio are engaged

in this same "strict and most observant watch."
Marcellus and Bernardo are not common sentries.
They are gentlemen and scholars, who are on duty
as soldiers for this particular occasion.   Lines 140
to 142 I should also like to see inserted, because
they are needed to explain the words which follow—

> "We do it wrong, being so majestical,
> To offer it this show of violence."

On the stage these words are spoken, but no violence
is shown towards the Ghost.   Besides, the business
of striking at the Ghost is a fine invention of the
author to assist the imagination to realize it is
a spirit.   I am sorry lines 157 to 165 are omitted,
because not only are they beautiful in themselves,
but also appropriate, for they help to give solemnity
to the scene.   The omission of the last four lines of
the scene leaves it unfinished.   Altogether seventy-
one lines have been cut out of the first scene, but
the first quarto retains most of them.

The stage-directions at the head of the second
scene, both in the Globe edition and folio, place
Hamlet's name after the Queen's, to indicate the
order to be observed by the actors when they come
on to the stage.   In the second quarto, however,
Hamlet's name comes last.   As he has an antipathy
to the King, and is displeased with his mother, it
is not likely he would be much in the company of
either, not even on State occasions, for Hamlet
regards the King as a usurper.   I would venture to
suggest, then, that Hamlet should enter last of all,
from another doorway to that used by the King
and his train, having his hat and cloak in his hand,
as if he had come to take leave of the Court before
starting for Wittenberg.

Passing on now to the fourth scene, I notice that in the acting-edition the last five lines of the scene have been cut out, including that expressive one—

" Something is rotten in the state of Denmark."

I do not myself sympathize with this cutting out the end of scenes, as is done so persistently in every acted play of Shakespeare's. It is inartistic, because it is done to allow the principal actor to leave the stage with applause. Besides, it creates a habit, with actors, of trying to make points at the end of scenes, whether it is necessary or not, and this distorts the play and delays its progress.

In the fifth scene the line—

" O horrible, horrible, most horrible "—

spoken by the Ghost, is marked in the acting-edition to be spoken by Hamlet. Such an alteration is unwarranted by the text. The first quarto, by making Hamlet exclaim "O God" after the Ghost has said "O horrible," gives indication that the words " O horrible" were spoken on the Elizabethan stage by the Ghost.

An alteration has also been made in the Ghost's last line, which to some may appear a trivial matter. The folio attaches the word "Hamlet" to the "Adieu," and puts a colon between it and the words " Remember me," showing thereby that a slight pause should be made before these two last words are spoken, in order to make them more impressive ; and the first quarto gives the same reading. French's acting-version, however, tacks the name on to the " Remember me." Cumberland's version gives the reading of the second quarto, which I think the best—

"Adieu, adieu, adieu, Remember me."

The omission in all the stage-versions of Hamlet's lines addressed to the Ghost, beginning "Ha, ha, boy!" "Hic et ubique?" "Well said, old Mole!" is, I think, not judicious, because it causes some actors to misconceive Shakespeare's intention in this scene. One can hardly read the authorized text without feeling that Hamlet is here shown as a young man, or, perhaps, a "boy," as his mother calls him, in the first quarto, thrown into the intensest excitement. His delicate, nervous temperament has undergone a terrible shock from the interview with the Ghost, yet, owing to the absence of these lines, our Hamlets on the stage finish this scene with the most dignified composure. From the first act 217 lines have been omitted in French's acting-edition.

In the beginning of the second act the scene between Polonius and Reynaldo is left out in all the acting-versions. It is a very amusing scene, and in my opinion gives a better insight into the character of Polonius than any of the others. If it were inserted I believe it would become popular with the audience, and we find it retained in the first quarto. The second scene is called "*A Room in the Castle*" both in the Globe and acting editions. Might it not be an exterior scene? It is true that Polonius remarks "Here in the lobby," but the line next to this in the first quarto suggests that he is pointing to some place off the scene, for he adds "There let Ophelia walk," and Ophelia is on the stage. An exterior scene would, in my opinion, give more meaning to the words "Will you walk out of the air, my lord?"

and to Hamlet's speech, "This most excellent canopy the air," etc. The scene of a palace garden or cloister could be well introduced in a play so full of interiors. It would add to the interest of the scene if Hamlet took advantage of the early entrance in the quarto and in the folio. For Hamlet to catch sight of Polonius hurrying the King and Queen off the scene would account for his suspicions and explain his rudeness to Polonius. Lines 374 to 378, Globe edition, are omitted in the acting-edition, but should surely be inserted, because they are needed to explain why Hamlet's reception of Rosencrantz and Guildenstern when they first enter, differs from that of the Players. I have always thought that the Hamlets of our stage, not being familiar with the context, mistake Shakespeare's intention. I gather from the omitted lines that Hamlet should warmly welcome the players, and take them by the hand.

At line 381, in the Globe edition, Polonius is marked to enter and speak on the stage the line "Well be with you, gentlemen." In the acting-edition he is marked to speak this "*without*" (to whom? certainly not to the players; Polonius would not have addressed them in such terms), and to enter at a cue lower down the page. The alteration is an instance of what I consider the wrong principle adopted in making stage-versions. The actors have preferred thinking Shakespeare wrong to using a little ingenuity to meet his stage-directions. They have said: " It will never do to have Polonius stand still saying nothing while Hamlet is making fun of him to Rosencrantz and Guildenstern, so he must speak his line off the stage." Would it not have shown more consideration for the author's text to make Polonius enter where directed, and then find something for him to do after he is on the stage ? For instance, he might enter from a side entrance, as if summoned by the sound of the trumpet, move hastily towards the back of the stage, where the new-comers would arrive, and .greet Hamlet, Rosencrantz, and Guildenstern, as he passes them, with the words, " Well be with you, gentlemen."

The wording in the acting-version of the stage-direction, "*Enter four or five* Players *and two* Actresses," is questionable. Perhaps it is not a matter of great consequence, unless the period chosen for representation be the Elizabethan one, and I would suggest that this is the most appropriate period for the play, because to adopt an early Danish period is contradictory to the text, and overloads the piece with material foreign to the author's intentions. Shakespeare's thoughts were not in Denmark when he wrote this play.

Hamlet's recitation of Priam's slaughter in the acting-version has been cut down from thirteen to three lines, and I venture to think unwisely. Hamlet has chosen these lines because they express in biting words his contempt for the King, his uncle, and the audience should become aware of this by the marked emphasis Hamlet lays on each epithet applied to Pyrrhus.

I am sorry that Hamlet's line to the Player, " He's for a jig, or a tale of bawdry, or else he sleeps," has been cut out. Besides being a fine hit at Polonius, it is an instructive piece of sarcasm. Playgoers in the twentieth century need as much to be told the truth as those in the sixteenth.

In Cumberland's acting version the editor has inserted the stage-direction—"*pointing to Hamlet*" —before Polonius speaks his line, "Look whether he hath not changed colour," etc. I believe this is the right reading, although it is not the one usually adopted on the stage. If Polonius had been speaking the words to Hamlet with reference to the player he surely would have inserted the words "my lord." Besides, these manifestations of grief are more likely to arouse sympathy in Polonius coming from the " mad " Hamlet than from the actor, whose business it was to simulate emotion. By the way, the skill of this play-actor seems to have been underrated on our stage. Actors are always considered at liberty to rant the part, but from Hamlet's description of his performance he should be an executant of considerable ability. It is curious that in Oxberry's acting-edition the first half of Hamlet's closing soliloquy is omitted, and he begins at the line, "I have heard that guilty creatures," etc.; showing that even a great actor such as Edmund Kean could take some unpardonable liberties with his author. Two hundred and thirty-eight lines have been omitted from the second act of the stage-version.

The first scene in the third act is called in French's acting-edition, "*A Room in the Castle as prepared for the Play,*" and in Cumberland's, "*A Hall in the Palace, Theatre in the Background.*" But the interview between Ophelia and Hamlet should take place in the lobby spoken of by Polonius, the play being acted later in the day. It would add to the interest of the scene if the actor impersonating Hamlet availed himself of the position marked in the second quarto for his entrance, and actually saw the King and Polonius concealing themselves. Was not this Shakespeare's intention?

I notice, in Hamlet's soliloquy, that the folio has the expression, "the *poor* man's contumely." As the Globe edition, and, indeed, all the modern editions, retain the expression "proud," used in the second quarto, I suppose that the "poor man's contumely" is not considered a legitimate expression. It is curious, however, that the first quarto has an expression somewhat similar in meaning, "The rich man cursed of the poor." In "Twelfth Night," also, a play written not long before "Hamlet," Olivia says: "O world, how apt the poor are to be proud!"

In the scene with Ophelia and Hamlet, both in French's and Cumberland's acting-version, Hamlet is marked to exit after the word "Farewell," and to re-enter again directly afterwards, thus conveying the impression that he returns in order to give more force to his reproaches. These stage-directions are not to be found in either of the quartos or yet in the folio, and I can find no foundation for them in the text. They seem to me to be an unnecessary interruption in a solemn scene, and to interfere with its impressiveness. Hamlet is dismissing Ophelia to a nunnery, and the word "Farewell" is added to impress her with the necessity of her going. She must leave him, not he her. It is, indeed, a subtle touch of Shakespeare's that Ophelia here should think Hamlet's intense feeling and earnestness was madness, for the Prince was "hoist with his own petard," having previously assumed madness for the purpose of breaking off his engagement with her, "made in honourable fashion, with almost all the holy vows of heaven." After the exit of Polonius and the King, the stage-direction in the acting version is: "*Enter* Hamlet *and* First Player." The Globe edition makes this the beginning of another scene, and where changes of scene take place in a theatre it would be correct to make an alteration, for the scene in the text is a banqueting hall and the time night. The stage-direction of the second quarto gives, "*Enter* Hamlet *and three of the* Players," and that of the folio, "*Enter* Hamlet *and two or three of the* Players." Hamlet, therefore, should not enter, as he does now, with only one player.

I should like to make a remark in passing on Hamlet's expression, "trippingly on the tongue." If Burbage's company spoke Shakespeare's lines in this way, I believe the longer plays could be acted in three hours. The late Mr. Brandram's recitals showed how much more effective Shakespeare's lines can be made when spoken "trippingly on the tongue," and that the enjoyment of the public depends more upon the appropriate rendering of the text than upon the scenic accessories.

The stage-direction in the folio for the entrance of the court to see the play reads: "*Enter* King, *etc., with his guard carrying torches.*" It is a pity, I think, that these directions are not inserted in our acting versions. It would make a pretty picture for the stage to be darkened, and to have the mimic play acted by torchlight.

The "*dumb-show*" is omitted in all the stage-versions, and is not represented on the stage, but I think the play-scene is imperfectly realized by leaving it out. The Queen's reply to Hamlet's

question, "Madame, how like you the play?" and
the King's inquiry, "Have you heard the argument?
Is there no offence in it?" would have a deeper
significance with it represented; for evidently the
poisoning in the "*dumb show*" has made no impression on the Queen, but a very marked one on the
King, and Hamlet's reply, "poison in jest," assumes
quite a different meaning. Besides, Hamlet's words,
"The croaking raven doth bellow for revenge,"
shows that he already has become convinced of the
King's guilt before the appearance of Lucianus—and
how, except by means of the "*dumb show*"? I believe,
too, that if it were represented, then the mistake many
actors fall into of making a climax at the lines, "He
poisons him in the garden," etc., and speaking them
to the King, and not to his courtiers, would be
corrected. There seems no justification for Hamlet
making a climax of these lines. It is anticipating
the King's exit, which is the last thing Hamlet would
wish for. He tells the court that it shall see "*anon*"
how the murderer will marry the wife of Gonzago,
and the King defeats his nephew's purpose by stop-
ping the play. Hamlet's most dramatic line in this
scene, one at which a point might be legitimately
made, is cut out in the acting-version. Ophelia
says, "The King rises." Then Hamlet exclaims,
"What! frighted with *false* fire!" Also the Queen's
remark to her husband, "How fares my lord?" has
been omitted. The words have some value as
evidence of the Queen's ignorance of the King's
crime. If she knew of it the question was
unnecessary.

"*Exit Horatio*" is the stage-direction in the acting-
edition, after Hamlet's words, "Come, some music;"

but there is no similar stage-direction in either the second quarto or folio. Later on, in the acting-edition, comes the direction: "*Enter* Horatio *with* Recorders." In the second quarto it is, "*Enter the Players with recorders*," and in the folio, "*Enter one with a recorder.*" It seems just possible that Hamlet's lines—

> "Ah ! ha ! come, some music ; come, the recorders.
> For if the King like not the tragedy,
> Why, then, belike he likes it not, perdy "—

may not be said to Horatio at all, but to one of the players who may be hanging about the stage waiting for instructions after the sudden interruption of the performance. He would then retire, and send some of his fellows with recorders. In French's acting-edition the words, "To withdraw with you," are altered to "So withdraw with you," after which comes the rather curious stage-direction, "*Exeunt* Horatio *and* Recorders." There are no such directions in the quartos or folio. A recorder is not a person, but a musical instrument. From indications in the first quarto, Horatio should remain on the stage until the end of the scene, for Hamlet says, "Good-night, Horatio," to which Horatio replies, "Good-night unto your lordship."

The third scene in the Globe edition is the second scene in the acting-version. French's edition contains the King's long soliloquy, and omits Hamlet's entrance. Cumberland's edition omits both. I think that to omit Hamlet's entrance in this scene is to interfere with Shakespeare's dramatic construction. Its omission breaks an important link between the closet scene and the play scene, and prevents the audience fully realizing the consequences of Hamlet's clemency. Shakespeare shows us Hamlet wishing to take the King's life at three different periods during the play, but the King's craft and Hamlet's conscience stand in the way; for the Ghost's word must first be challenged; then the mother's wishes must be respected; while the King's prayers must not be interrupted; and when the next opportunity occurs the wrong man is killed. This is the sequence of the story, and it should not be broken; even the compiler of the first quarto knew this, for all three incidents are made prominent in his text. But our stage Hamlets try to tone down the inconsistencies and imperfections of the character; they exploit his sentiments, but do not show his inclinations. Hamlet wants to kill the King, notwithstanding that his sensitive nature instinctively rebels against the deed. A student, a controversialist, and a moralist, what has he to do with revenge or murder? But Hamlet, regardless of his own temperament, thinks only of his duty to his father.

Passing now to the third scene, which is the fourth in the Globe edition, I find that after the exit of the Ghost no less than 52 lines have been cut out, and their omission has caused actors to introduce stage-business which is contradictory to the text. Many Hamlets show an emotional tenderness towards the Queen which would be quite out of place if all the text were spoken. Look at the fierce satire expressed in lines 190 onwards! Hamlet in his self-constituted office "as scourge and minister" cannot caress his mother or hold her in his arms as is now done by actors. However much she may solicit his sympathy, his reply is: "I must be cruel only to be kind."

I should like to see inserted in the acting-edition the fine lines of Hamlet to the Queen—

> " Forgive me this my virtue,
> For in the fatness of these pursy times
> Virtue itself of vice must pardon beg,
> Yea, curb and woo, for leave to do him good."

From the third act 216 lines have been omitted.

The fourth act on the stage sometimes begins with the fifth scene, Globe edition, but very often the first and the third scenes are acted. These scenes seem to belong to the third act. They take place the same night, and are a continuation of the closet scene, for in the first quarto and folio the Queen is not marked to go off, but the King to enter after Hamlet's exit. Between the fourth and fifth scenes a pause can well take place to allow of Laertes' return from France. This addition to the third act would make it very long, unless the Hamlet and Ophelia scene were made part of the second act, bringing down the curtain on the words, "Madness in great ones must not unwatched go." Two objections to this suggestion, however, can be urged owing to the lapse of a day between the second and third acts, and the bringing together of Hamlet's two long soliloquies. But an interval is only needed to show that time has been allowed to prepare the play, and, therefore, can come as well after the scene with Ophelia as before; and a good actor would surmount the difficulty of the two soliloquies by varying the delivery of each. This revision of act-intervals would make the construction of the play resemble more that of the first quarto, which, for acting purposes, is certainly the better version of the two. Moreover, in the folio

there appear no divisions beyond the second act,
nor any indications in the text to show where
Shakespeare may have wished another pause to
come in the representation.

In the first scene of the fourth act, Globe edition,
the Queen, speaking of Hamlet, says :

> " To draw apart the body he hath killed,
>   O'er whom his very madness, like some ore
>   Among a mineral of metals base,
>   Shows itself pure ; he weeps for what is done."

These lines are omitted in the acting-versions.
Perhaps, if they were inserted, many actors might
consider it necessary to show more concern for the
death of Polonius than has hitherto been the stage
practice.

The fifth scene, Globe edition, is the second scene
in French's, and the fourth in Cumberland's. I think
it would add to the dignity of Horatio's character
if, as directed in the second quarto, the Queen and
Horatio entered with "a gentleman," who brings
news of Ophelia's mental derangement. Horatio
is not a servant, nor even a gentleman-in-waiting ;
but a visitor from Wittenberg. The Queen, having
lost her son, would naturally seek the society of
his bosom friend. The stage-direction in the first
quarto for Ophelia's entrance should be noticed ;
I should like to see it inserted in the acting-edition :
" *Enter* Ophelia *playing on a lute, with her hair hanging down, singing.*" This, no doubt, is how she
appeared on Burbage's stage. I can imagine
Ophelia entering as if she were wandering about
the corridors of the palace singing and muttering to
herself unconscious of what she was saying, where
she was going, or to whom she was speaking ; the

imbecility of a pretty young girl who had been, at one time, fond of her songs as of her sewing. In the acting-edition the stage-direction for the second entrance describes her as being *"fantastically dressed with straws and flowers,"* but there is no similar direction in the quartos or folio. Ophelia has very little time allowed her to go anywhere, and certainly not beyond the palace precincts, where she might not find straws or daisies. Shakespeare may have intended the flowers to be imaginary ones to which she refers that the audience may anticipate her ramble beyond the palace to make garlands in the meadows. Songs were rarely sung on the stage unaccompanied, and it must be remembered that Ophelia was a court lady, more accustomed to handle the lute than to pick wild-flowers. The third scene of the fourth act, being the fifth scene in the Globe edition, I have never seen acted on the stage. The omission is, perhaps, not important, except that the spectators are left ignorant as to the cause of Hamlet's return. From the fourth act 303 lines have been omitted in the acting-version.

Coming now to the fifth act, the stage-direction for Ophelia's burial, both in the Globe and acting-editions, is as follows: *"Enter* Priests, *etc., in Procession, the corpse of* Ophelia, Laertes, *and* Mourners *following,* King, Queen, *their Trains, etc."* This direction is hardly consistent with Hamlet's description, "Such maimed rites." I should prefer the direction in the first quarto: *"Enter* King *and* Queen, Laertes *and other* Lords, *with a* Priest *after the coffin."* The absence of religious ceremony should attract the attention of the audience as much as it does Hamlet's.   I should like to see only *one* Priest present, and the coffin borne by soldiers or villagers, not by monks or nuns.   It is often the stage practice for the Priest to stand over the grave with a book in his hand and intone his lines (replies to Laertes' questions) as if they were part of the burial service.   A rather erroneous conception of Shakespeare's churlish Priest, who objects to the funeral taking place on sacred ground, and refuses even to approach the grave.

In the first quarto, at the words " What's he that conjures so," is written the stage-direction, " Hamlet *leaps in after* Laertes," and I find that Oxberry's edition has the same direction, only inserted a little lower down.   I presume, therefore, that the elder Kean did actually leap into the grave.   Our modern Hamlets would object to this business as undignified, and perhaps it is ; but, at the same time, Hamlet's public apology to Laertes in the last scene requires some marked movement of his in this scene.   He owns himself that he was in a towering passion.   Laertes may handle Hamlet roughly, but not till Hamlet has interfered with him.

None of our stage Hamlets appear in the church-yard in any change of costume.   From the familiar way in which the clown talks to Hamlet, and Hamlet's declaration, " Behold, 'tis I, Hamlet, the Dane," I imagine that Shakespeare intended Hamlet to be dressed in some disguise in this scene.   When Hamlet, writing to the King, says, " Naked and alone," he may not only mean unarmed, but stripped of his fine clothes, so that it would not be inappropriate for him to appear at the grave in some common sailor's dress.   In the second scene in this act Hamlet says, "With my sea-gown scarf'd about me," a line that also would furnish some excuse for change of costume. Both in the first quarto and the folio the lines, "This is mere madness," etc., are spoken by the King. The acting-edition follows the second quarto, and gives the lines to the Queen. The King had good reason to impress upon others the belief that Hamlet is mad; and when the villagers hear the taunt they should shun the lunatic.

The second scene is divided in the stage-version; and now that it has become the custom to lower the curtain for each change of scene, I would suggest that the churchyard-scene be changed at once to the hall where the duel takes place. The forcing of this duel upon Hamlet by the King would be better shown by the King and all the court coming down to Hamlet than Hamlet's going to them. It is the difference between his going to meet death and death coming to him.

In this second scene of the acting-edition there is a line of the King's omitted, which, perhaps, if it were inserted, would cause an alteration in the stage-business connected with it. The King says: "Give me the cups," showing that more than one cup is brought to the King, one of them, probably, containing the poison. In this cup the King places his jewel, to insure Hamlet's drinking out of it. On the stage it is the common practice to use only one cup, and to imagine that the pearl contains the poison.

I have before expressed my regret that the play should end at Hamlet's death. Shakespeare would have considered the play unfinished, and even the partisans of stage effect would lose nothing by

the introduction of Fortinbras. The distant sound
of the drum, the tramp of soldiers, the gradual
filling of the stage with them, the shouts of the
crowd outside, the chieftain's entrance fresh from his
victories, and the tender, melancholy young prince,
dead in the arms of his beloved friend, are material
for a fine picture, a strong dramatic contrast. Life
in the midst of death! Was not this Shakespeare's
conception? From the last act 219 lines have been
omitted.

The acting-editions of Shakespeare's plays are
worth examining by students in order to ascertain
how far they are consistent with the author's intention. Since the chronological order of the plays
has been fixed with more or less certainty, the study
of Shakespeare has become much easier, and his
dramatic and poetical conceptions are more accurately realized than they ever were before. The
time has now come when our acting-editions could
be profitably revised. Eminent actors may prefer,
perhaps, arranging versions from their own study
of the text, but there must always exist a standard
version for general use in the profession. I should
like to see existing a playbook of "Hamlet" which
has been altered and shortened by a joint board
of actors and scholars. It should have a carefully
written introduction describing minutely the play
as it is believed the author conceived it. There
should also be a short sketch of the persons represented, with hints to the actor where to look in
omitted passages for glimpses of character; besides
notes on obscure passages, unfamiliar expressions,
and different readings; and a description of cos-

tume and scenery most appropriate to the play. Such a book might be the beginning of a new era for the Shakespearian drama on our stage, and, by stimulating actors to study their parts from an artistic point of view, and less from a theatrical one, it would enable the public to appreciate Shakespeare in the only place where he can be properly understood, and that is the theatre.

"KING LEAR."*

When I opened the newspapers to read the criticisms on a recent performance of "King Lear," and found that the first comments made were in praise of the costumes, the scenery, and the music, then I knew that once more Shakespeare and tragedy had failed to assert themselves in the English Theatre. Charlotte Brontë, the novelist, who was educated in Brussels, and saw Rachel in one of her greatest impersonations, once astounded a London dinner-party by saying that the English knew nothing about tragedy. In her diary she writes : " I have twice seen Macready act, once in ' Macbeth' and once in ' Othello.' It is the fashion to rave about his splendid acting ; anything more false and artificial, less genuinely impressive than his whole style, I could scarcely have imagined. The fact is the stage system is altogether hollow nonsense. They act farces well enough ; the actors comprehend their parts and do justice to them. They comprehend nothing about tragedy or Shakespeare, and it is a failure. I said so, and by so

* *The New Age*, September, 1909.

saying produced a blank silence, a mute consterna-
tion." Unfortunately, Charlotte Brontë's reproach
still remains true. Perhaps, had she continued to
protest, the public would then have recognized the
truth of her remarks. As it was, she never again
referred to the subject. Like most of our literary
men and women, then and now, she preferred to
remain discreetly silent upon all matters connected
with Shakespeare and the stage.

Last night, in a London theatre, Charlotte Brontë's
words were forcibly brought back to my mind.
I have once seen a great rendering of the part
of Lear, but it was given by an Italian, Signor
Rossi. I have seen the whole play correctly
rendered, with every character a vivid realization
of the poet's conception, but this was at a performance in the Court Theatre at Munich. For thirty
years I have been a constant playgoer, and seen the
best art this country can produce, but never can I
say that I have seen English tragedy on the English
stage. The cause is not far to seek. We have actors
in abundance, and some of them creative artists ;
yet we have no tragic actors, because we have no
school in which to develop them. Until we can set
apart a theatre for the exclusive use of classical
drama and its interpreters, we cannot hope to have
tragedy finely acted. A tragedy in verse is the
severest test of the artist's powers, of his physical
flexibility in voice and face, of his training and
sensibility. When, therefore, I heard who was
going to essay the greatest tragic rôle that has ever
been written, the result was a foregone conclusion :
exit Shakespeare and enter the Producer.

Yes! He is the hero of the moment, as all our

newspapers have told us, only it is unfortunate, in the interests of art, that to the praise there should have been added no discernment. Macaulay has said that the sure sign of the general decline of an art is the frequent occurrence, not of deformity, but of misplaced beauty, and whatever beauty has been put into the production is undoubtedly misplaced. We can accept accuracy in scenery and costume when the play itself is historically accurate —that is to say, when it has been written to show the difference between two periods as that of British and Norman, or when it defines some distinctive characteristic of race relating to its morals or manners. But what is there in "King Lear" that suggests such a remote period as 800 B.C. ? We are told in the programme that Shakespeare purposely removes the story from Christian times to give the tragedy its proper setting in "a remote age of barbarism, when man in wanton violence was at war with Nature." The story, however, belongs to one of the popular fables of European literature. Like "Cinderella," it was in all probability transplanted into our country from a foreign source. In its application it is universal, and marks no special epoch or nationality, nor is there in the story or its characters anything out of keeping with a Christian age. Have there been no ungrateful daughters, no adulterers, no bastards, no tyrants, no jealous lovers since the years B.C.? The motive for crime remains pretty much the same to-day as it did before the Christian era, and will continue to remain the same until the economic conditions of human existence are readjusted. It is contrary to history and experience to suppose that in Shakespeare's time dramatists deliberately aimed at illustrating not only the customs but also the morals of a barbaric age. If we do not to-day tear out the eyes of our enemy, it is because we have discovered some less clumsy way of revenging our injuries. But because our manners are more refined, it does not follow that our morals are purer. The story of " King Lear," as Shakespeare has set it forth, is one that may happen to-day in any kingdom and any home. This is what the producer has failed to grasp, and why his scenes and costumes do not illustrate his play.

Throughout the performance the spectators' eyes are at variance with the spoken words. Did the early Britons have stocks ? Were there such persons as marshals, heralds, knights, drums, and colours ? Did beldames walk the villages, and were there wakes and fairs in market-towns? Why was fish eaten on Fridays ? Had " Bessy " crossed the bourn ? How did the ballads become known a thousand years before they were written? Needlessly is the attention distracted by these anachronisms which upset the spectator's equanimity in a play that is pulsating with ever-living human emotion. Then, again, costume is an essential adjunct in drama, as an indication of character. We know at a glance a man's rank, his wealth, and his taste, by the aid of his clothes, provided always that we are familiar with the period in which the apparel was worn. But put the men into bath-sheets or into night-shirts, and we cannot tell the master from the servant. As a fact the producer has put all his characters into dressing-gowns—showy ones, doubtless —while the hair of the men is as long as that of the women. In vain do we seek among these sexless creatures for our familiar characters, to know who is who. Where is the king, the earl, the peasant, the knave, the soldier, the civilian ? There are slight distinctions in the costumes worn by these characters, but to the uninitiated they are meaningless. Infinite variety in character and situation is created by the author, and none shown by the producer owing to the choice of an archaic period. How the spectator longs for sight of the fool's cap, bells and bauble, of the herald's tabard, and the knight's armour ; to see a girl as a girl, and a man as a man, and to know which is the lady and which the queen !

A country squire, whose hobby was horses, once told me that although at twenty he thought himself a good judge of a thoroughbred, after fifty more years of experience he hesitated a long while in determining a nag's good points. It is the same with the student of Shakespeare ; the oftener he has read one of the poet's plays, and the more study he has given to it, the longer he hesitates to criticize. The art of the dramatist is too thorough and too subtle to be lightly discussed. To all stage-managers who wish to mend or improve Shakespeare I say : " Hands off ! Produce this play as it is written or leave it alone. Don't take liberties with it ; the man who does that does not understand his own limitations !" Let us uphold that there is but one rule to be followed when it becomes necessary to shorten one of the poet's plays ; and that is to omit lines, but never an entire scene. Shakespeare, of all his contemporaries, unless it be Ford, gave to his dramas—especially to his later ones—unity of design; so that each scene has a relation to the whole play. But in the preparation of this stage-version of "King Lear" it must be admitted that no rule, no method, no love, nor respect has been shown; and, what is the least pardonable fault, no knowledge is apparent. Scenes and passages have been torn out of the play, just as children might tear up bank-notes, regardless of the value of the parts to the whole. No matter if the story to modern minds is unintelligible, the characters incoherent, and the ethics of the play unconvincing, the management presumes that, as everything in "King Lear" took place among the early Britons, eight hundred years before Christ, only the costumes and scenery of the producer can be expected to elucidate the barbarities of the play or its people.

Stowed away in an odd corner of the drama, Shakespeare generally introduces some words to indicate his point of view, and, in regard to "King Lear," his view is thus expressed:

"EDMUND: This is the excellent foppery of the world, that, when we are sick in fortune [often the surfeit of our own behaviour], we make guilty of our disasters the sun, the moon, and stars; as if we were villains by necessity; fools by heavenly compulsion . . . and all that we are evil in, by divine thrusting on" (Act I., Scene 2).

And Shakespeare repeats the warning in "Coriolanus":

"The gods be good unto us! . . . No, in such a case the gods will not be good unto us," etc. (Act V., Scene 4).

Now, unfortunately, Edmund's speech is omitted from the stage-version, so that the playgoer who does not know his Shakespeare misses the irony of the terrible tragedy he is called upon to witness. The poet wishes us to understand that if a community leaves to the care of the gods man's responsibility to his fellow-men, instead of taking that responsibility upon itself, then life will go on to-day—and does go on—just as it did in the age of Elizabeth. All through the play Shakespeare denies omnipotence to man's self-made gods. Edmund has good looks, intelligence, and good intentions (Act I., Scene 2). The community, however, in which he lives decides that because he is an illegitimate child these gifts shall not be profitably employed for the good of the State or for the benefit of the individual who possesses them. Edmund therefore becomes embittered, and revenges himself upon that community. Goneril, Regan, and Cornwall, being vicious in mind and self-seeking, make use of Edmund's abilities to serve their own ends, by which means the catastrophe in the death of Cordelia and Lear is brought about, together with the deaths of the plotters. But Kent, Albany, Gloucester, and Edgar believe that all their misfortunes are brought about by the gods. Well, perhaps they are, if we admit that by the gods is meant society's instinct for self-preservation, which compels it to rebel against bad laws and bad conventions. Unfortunately, however, history shows that a community can live too much in awe of its self-imposed gods, who overrule natural instinct, and encourage ignorance and folly, when a nation soon perishes, and is wiped out of existence.

It has been said that the putting out of Gloucester's eyes is an artistic mistake on Shakespeare's part. I hold that it is a necessary incident in the play, and that the dramatist has shown the reason for it. Cordelia has set foot in the country with her French soldiers, determined to regain the kingdom for her father, and Gloucester, whom Cornwall regards as belonging to his own faction, is conniving with Cordelia. Now had Gloucester been a common soldier, Cornwall could have put him to death as a traitor (Act III., Scene 7); but the offender being an earl, Cornwall dare not do this, so he puts out the old man's eyes to prevent him reading Cordelia's despatches. He is blinded, moreover, in sight of the audience, that Cornwall may be seen receiving his death-wound. And even the fact that Regan and Goneril were capable of acting so inhumanly towards Gloucester makes Lear's plight more desperate, and therefore more pathetic. Yet Shakespeare never makes his characters suffer without giving them compensations, and the meeting and reconciliation between the blind Gloucester and his son is one of the most touching incidents in the play. That this reconciliation was omitted in representation suggests that the ugly incident of putting out Gloucester's eyes was retained merely as a piece of sensationalism, and, if so, it merits severe condemnation.

Shakespeare has often been blamed for being intolerant to democracy, and this is in part a well-founded reproach, but it was a fault of the age and not of the man. Still, in "King Lear" the dramatist abundantly proves his sympathy with the hard lot of the poor. For this reason the play preaches no pessimism. Lear, Gloucester, and Edgar are the happier for the troubles they experience. Such hardships as they endure are brought upon themselves by their own shortcomings; but these hardships are mitigated by the gain to their moral natures of a fellow-sympathy for the sufferings of those who have done no wrong, and by an appreciation of the injustice done towards those whose miseries are created through the selfishness of the rich. Lear, who has ruled a country as a despot for half a century, discovers for the first time in his life that—

"Through tattered clothes small vices do appear; Robes and furred gowns hide all."

Having exposed himself to feel what wretches feel, he knows, as he has never known before, how the heart of a desolate father can crave for the love of a gentle daughter. To prison he can cheerfully go with her,

"To pray and sing and tell old tales, and laugh at gilded butter-flies,"

because now he is no longer himself in the wrong, but the one who is wronged. And the blind Gloucester, also, is happy in his misery, because for the first time he can say:

> "Let the superfluous and lust-dieted man ;—
>   that will not see
> Because he does not feel, feel your power quickly ;
> So distribution should undo excess,
> And each man have enough."

This is Shakespeare's message to the aristocracy to-day, and yet all this is cut out by the actor-manager who seems to imagine that these sentiments are barbaric, and only represent the opinions of men who lived some three thousand years ago.

The omissions in this stage-version are in a great measure due to carelessness in the study of the play

The right point of view from which to present this colossal tragedy on the stage has been missed, and the stage-manager having allowed his actors to take up half the evening in drawling out the words of the first two acts, the blue pencil has been used for the remaining three with a freedom and ignorance which never should have been sanctioned.

" *Matinées* every Wednesday and Saturday." These words appear on all printed bills announcing the performance of " King Lear." They go far to explain why the play fails to represent tragedy either in its emotion or terror, and why it sends play-goers back to their homes as cold and indifferent to human suffering as it left them. What is offered to the public is a kinematograph show ; walking figures who gesticulate and utter human sounds ; puppets who mechanically move through their parts conscious that the business must be done all over again within a few hours. Does an actor honestly think that he can impersonate Lear's hysterical passion, madness, and death, twice in a day, and day by day, and that he can do this efficiently together with all his other duties of management ? That he may wish to do so is intelligible, but that the public should sanction it and the critics tolerate it is strange indeed. That the exigencies of modern theatrical management impose these conditions is beside the question. A less exacting play might have been chosen instead of distorting one of Shakespeare's masterpieces. Salvini, whose reputation as a tragedian is universally acknowledged, refused to act Othello more than three times in a week, and never on two consecutive days; and those who saw his moving performance must admit that it was a physical impossibility for him to do otherwise. A man does not suffer the tortures of jealousy without physical and mental prostration; and the actor endures a very heavy strain when he seeks to simulate an emotion which has not been aroused in a natural way.

The actor, however, not only fails to reproduce the emotions of Lear, he never even shows us the outside of the man. We look in vain about the stage to find the King; instead we see a decrepit, commonplace old man, though Lear is neither the one nor the other. He should resemble an English hunting "squarson," a man overflowing with vitality, who is as hale and active at eighty as he was at forty; a large-hearted, good-natured giant, with a face as red as a lobster. He is one of the spoilt children of nature, spoilt by reason of his favoured position in life. Responsible to no one, he thinks himself omnipotent. No one but Lear must be "fiery," no one but him unreasonable or contrary. In the crushing of this strong, unyielding, but lovable personality lies the drama of the play: this is what an Elizabethan audience went to the Globe Playhouse to see. But how can the story be told when a Lear comes on the stage, who at his *first* appearance is broken-down and half-witted? Where is the purpose or the art in showing us such a helpless creature being ill-treated by his own kindred? Yet Lear boasts of his physical strength; and how skilfully the dramatist has planned the entrance, so as to accentuate the virility of the man! The play opens with prose, and the first line of verse is spoken by the King, so that the change of rhythm may the better call attention to his entrance. Those who saw Signor Rossi, in the part, dart on to the stage, and with a voice of commanding authority utter the words—

" *Attend* the lords of France and Burgundy, Gloster "—

recognized the Lear of Shakespeare. This single line, as by a flash of lightning, revealed the impetuosity and imperious disposition of the King, and prepared us for the volcanic disturbance that followed the thwarting of his will. Another thing, overlooked by all our English actors, is the necessity for Lear to come on the stage with Cordelia. On her first appearance she should be seen with her father in affectionate companionship, so as to balance with the last scene, where she is carried on in his devoted arms. Lear's division of his kingdom among his three daughters is not so eccentric a proceeding as the critics would make out. The King needs an excuse for giving the largest portion to his youngest child, and he thinks the most plausible reason is a public acknowledgment of the bond of affection between them. But Cordelia's sense of modesty and self-respect have not been taken into account, and Lear, who never tolerates a rebuff, in a moment of temper upsets all his pre-arranged plans, with disastrous consequence to himself and others. All this animated drama is omitted in the present performance, because Lear, on his first entrance, fails to give the keynote to the character or to the tragedy. Lear, in fact, is never seen on the stage, but only a Piccadilly actor who assumes the part, divested of frock coat and top hat.

The title-rôle, unfortunately, is not the only part

which has been wrongly cast. With the exception of Goneril and Regan, every character has been falsified and distorted. This is not due to want of ability in the actors, but to their physical limitations and to deficiency in training. Their reputations have been won in modern plays, and they seem quite unable to give expression to character when the medium of speech is verse. To those who think more about the actor than about the character he represents this is perhaps not a matter of much moment, but it is one of considerable importance to the play, since with all great dramatists the incidents are evolved by the characters; and if the men and women we see on the stage are not those that Shakespeare drew, his incidents are apt to appear ill-timed and ridiculous. After the title-rôle the most serious misconception of character is in the part of Edmund, the man whose wits control the movement of the drama. He is an offspring of the Italian Renaissance, a portrait of Machiavel's Prince, whose merit consists in his mental and physical fitness. He should be the handsomest man in the play, the most alert, the most able; he is a victim neither to sentimentality nor to self-deception, and he is fully capable of turning the weakness of others to his own advantage. It is impossible to hate the well-bred young schemer, because he is too clever, and his dupes are too silly. Unfortunately, the actor who is cast for this important part is quite unsuited for it. Another brilliant part which has suffered badly at the hands of its interpreter is Edgar, a character in which the Elizabethans delighted, because of its variety and the scope it allows for effective character-impersonation. The actor has to assume four parts—Edgar, an imbecile beggar, a peasant, and a knight-errant, and each of these characters should be a distinct creation; but the actor gave us nothing but a modern young man making himself unintelligibly ridiculous. Even more disastrous was the casting of the part of the fool, that gentle, frail lad who perishes from exposure to the storm, a child with the wisdom of a child, which is often the profoundest wisdom. Then a lady with a majestic figure cannot represent the little Cordelia, and she should not have been given the part. Of course the obvious retort to this kind of criticism is that the play must be cast from a company selected for repertory work, most of which, perhaps, will be modern. London managers, also, impose actors on the public because they have a London reputation, and this creates a monopoly which bc-comes a tyranny upon art. Whether the artist is suited or not for the part, he must be put into it, for box-office considerations.

To sum up. For the first time in the history of our stage the theatre is put under the management of a literary director, presumably with a view to bringing scholarly intelligence to bear upon the exponents of drama; but the result to the public, in so far as "King Lear" is concerned, is that it gets quite the most chaotic interpretation of the poet's work that it has ever been my misfortune to see represented on the stage. What is the reason? Has the director, like the fly, walked into the spider's parlour, or, in other words, into the network of theatrical commercialism, to find his artistic soul silenced and himself bound? Time perhaps will show us!

IV

THE NATIONAL THEATRE

THE REPERTORY THEATRE.
THE ELIZABETHAN STAGE SOCIETY.
SHAKESPEARE AT EARL'S COURT.
THE STUDENTS' THEATRE.
THE MEMORIAL SCHEME.

IV

A NATIONAL THEATRE

The Repertory Theatre.*

THE anxiety of dramatic critics to explain "the scant success" of Mr. Frohman's Repertory Theatre has created a large amount of paper argument, of more or less doubtful value, and now Mr. William Archer has added his view to that of others, and concludes his remarks with some practical advice to those who, in his opinion, are entitled to be regarded as "some of our ablest dramatists." The nature of this advice, however, is not only curious, but startling, when we recall the reception that was given to Ibsen's plays on their first appearance in this country, and remember that Mr. Archer was their warmest defender. Regardless of this defence, he now contends that "it is a grave misfortune for any writer, but it is a disaster for the dramatist, to get into the habit of despising popular taste and thinking that he has only himself to please in his writings."† But those who take their dramatic art seriously, and who wish their plays to have more than an ephemeral existence, cannot possibly accept this advice. They will recognize that the highest

* *The New Age*, November, 1910.

† *Fortnightly Review*, October, 1910, "The Theatrical Situation," by William Archer.

aim of a dramatist is to create a work valuable for all time, and that the most intimate knowledge of the moods and vagaries of playgoers cannot outweigh the smallest fault in the art of dramatic construction or character drawing. The conscientious artist repudiates the interference of public opinion with the expression of his art; he does not try to follow popular taste, but seeks to control and direct it. "The public," says George Sand, "is no artist; I will not tell you that we must please it, but we must win it. It winces, but gets over it." This is the advice Mr. Archer should have tendered to English playwrights, and let us hope it is the advice he meant to tender them. Nature has nowhere resigned her prerogative to the demands of popular taste, nor should the artist abandon his privileges. There is no record of a poet or musician having created a masterpiece through pandering to the "groundlings." Mozart, on completing an opera, would say: "I shall gain but little by this, but I have pleased myself, and that must be my recompense." It was Schiller who wrote: "My submission to the public convenience does not extend so far that I can allow any holes in my work and mutilate the characters of men." And Goethe exclaimed: "Nothing is more abhorrent to a reasonable man than an appeal to the majority." Lessing has said: "I have no objection to criticism condemning an artist, but it must not contaminate him. He must continue his work knowing that he is happier than his detractors." And Lessing points the moral in adding: "Genius is condemned to utter only absurdities when it is unfaithful to its mission." Bernard Shaw and Granville Barker, two of the able dramatists to whom Mr. Archer tenders his advice, have won "the ear of their contemporaries" equally with the more popular writers, Barrie and Maugham, and this they have done by the production of one or two plays which did not reach their hundredth performance. Euripides was none the less famous, as a dramatist, because the Athenian playgoers disliked his opinions and banished him from their midst. In fact, a dramatist is only great when he is able to dispense with the requirements of popular taste ; nor will he be satisfied with the knowledge that his play leaves some definite impression upon an audience unless it be that particular impression which belongs to tragedy, or comedy, or history, or pastoral drama, or conversational comedy.

Let it be, then, frankly admitted that a dramatist cannot both live in advance of the opinions of his audience and also reflect them. It is very well for Mr. Archer to talk about the vessel which does not float, but his illustration is surely less obvious than he imagines. A Noah's Ark will float on the ocean to-day as easily as it did in the days of the Flood, but no modern shipbuilder now would risk his reputation in constructing such a boat on the plea that it remains above water. Will the vessel weather the storms ? Will it outlive its competitors ? These are the vital questions in the art of both shipbuilding and playwriting.

Mr. Archer seems to forget that there is a prejudice among audiences as well as among individuals, and that every period of life has its own peculiar notions. Sometimes playgoers will receive an author's brightest comedy with coldness. The burden of Charles Lamb's reflections was—that the audience of his day came to the theatre to be complimented on its goodness. " The Stranger," " The Castle Spectre," and " George Barnwell," are specimens of the dramatic bill of fare which then found favour. On the other hand, the comic dramatists tried to disparage purity in men and women, and the sparkle of their comedies is unwholesome. In the opinion of many sober minds the dramatic literature of the Restoration is a blot upon our national history, while the gloomy productions that delighted the sentimental contemporaries of Charles Lamb are offences against dramatic art. At neither period was the drama national, in so far as it was representative of the tastes of all classes. Congreve and Wycherly wrote for the fashionable, while the admirers of Lillo's and Lewis's moral dramas were chiefly respectable shopkeepers. It was in Shakespeare's day that the nobility and groundlings together resorted to the playhouse, constituting themselves at once the patrons and pupils of the drama. The Elizabethan playgoer had no desire to bias the judgment of the dramatist. It left him free to represent life vividly and truly. It even encouraged him to be studious of the playgoer's profit as well as of his pleasure. But the playgoers of the Restoration, and of the period that immediately succeeded it, were intolerant of all views but their own. They regarded with disfavour plays which did not uphold their notions of amusement and morality. They called upon the dramatist to accept the opinion of his public, in these matters, as being superior to his own. As a consequence, the drama suffered in the attempt made to reconcile principles that are in themselves inconsistent, and the judgment of the audience was in no sense a criterion of merit in a play. This explains why some good plays have been coldly received on their first appearance. "She Stoops to Conquer" would have failed but for the presence in the theatre of Dr. Johnson and his friends ; Sheridan's "Rivals," an even more brilliant comedy, did not secure a fair hearing on its first performance. Of Diderot's comedy, the "Père de Famille," its author gives us the following information :

"And why did this piece, which nowadays fills the house before half-past four, and which the players always put up when they want a thousand crowns, have so lukewarm a welcome at first ?"

" . . . If I did not succeed at first it was because the style was new to the audience and actors ; because there was a strong prejudice, still existing, against what people call tearful comedy ; because I had a crowd of enemies at court, in town, among magistrates, among Churchmen, among men of letters."

"And how did you incur so much enmity ?"

"Upon my word, I don't know, for I have not written satires on great or small, and I have crossed no man on the path of fortune and dignities. It is true that I was one of the people called Philosophers, who were then viewed as dangerous citizens, and on whom the Government let loose two or three subalterns without virtue, without insight, and, what is worse, without talent. . . .

"To say nothing of the fact that these philosophers had made things more difficult for poets and men of letters in general, and that it was no longer possible to make oneself distinguished by knowing how to turn out a madrigal or a nasty couplet."*

This argument applies as forcibly to what goes on in the theatre in London to-day as it did in Paris nearly two hundred years ago. Perhaps, however, enough has been said to discount the suggestion

* "The Paradox of Acting," translated by Walter Herries Pollock.

that popular opinion is in any way responsible for the making of a good play.

M. Claretie once expressed a doubt if Englishmen quite understood the limitations of the French National Theatre ; because when the Comédie Française visited London in 1893, the Press (including Mr. Archer) ridiculed the intention of the director to give a more classical programme than English taste demanded, presumably forgetting that the selection of plays should be judged by an academic standard. The Comédie Française visited the Metropolis with a repertory apparently designed to illustrate the whole range of French dramatic literature, and yet, at the bidding of an exacting and ignorant public, it was called upon, without a protest from the critics, to withdraw the masterpieces of Molière and Racine in favour of the modern drama ; nor was it to the dignity of the Théâtre Française that its members consented to humour the caprices of playgoers, and condescended to bid for popularity when popularity meant bad taste and a craving for " stars." But the director, having entered into an arrangement with commercial gentlemen for commercial purposes, unexpectedly found himself compelled to forfeit his academic position, and to place his theatre on a level with a commercial playhouse. Fortunately the surrender did not serve its purpose. General dissatisfaction was expressed with the visit of the Comédie Française. The speculator lost his money, the playgoer did not see his " star," and the student heard no masterpieces.

Now, presumably, there is this difference between a National Theatre and a Repertory Theatre, that the object of the former is to keep before the public the best plays of the country, and those of other countries, and to give occasional performances of new plays of rare excellence and dignity. The Repertory Theatre, on the other hand, as we understand it in England, has for its task the exploiting of the new school of dramatists; of those men who have advanced ideas about their art and of the purpose it should serve. It is essentially, therefore, a theatre of experiment. If this is the case, and a manager such as Mr. Frohman cares to finance the undertaking, he can hardly be credited with considering the scheme in the light of a business speculation, nor would those dramatists who were invited to provide plays for this Repertory Theatre be expected to supply Mr. Frohman with the same class of work that they would submit to the ordinary theatrical manager. Here, evidently, is the opportunity, and the only opportunity a dramatist can get in this country, of providing a bill of fare capable of nourishing the weak intellects and the weaker susceptibilities of an audience. Looked at from this standpoint, it may be contended that no new play was produced under the Frohman Repertory management which did not advance the cause of dramatic art by adding to the knowledge of its author, to the experience of its actors, and to the education of the audience. "Misalliance" was a brilliant satire on modern society, one of the ripest conversational plays that Mr. Shaw's genius has yet produced; one in which the dramatist's observation probes deeper, and his wisdom and philosophy, as revealed in the play of character, are as subtle and less personal than anything Mr. Shaw, perhaps, has achieved hitherto in domestic drama. Why, then, are we now told that this play failed to attract, and with whom does the fault rest—is it with the author or his public? There was no insufficiency of "go," of wit, of raillery, of originality, or novelty; but there was, none the less, one thing wanting that to a modern audience is an unpardonable omission, and that is flattery. Society, as it lives to-day, under the maternal wing of the old lady in Stable Yard, expects to be humoured at the theatre, and to be complimented, not on its goodness, but on its vices. "Paint us as black as the devil," it says to the dramatist, "but don't dare to admit that we are a penny the worse because we are black!" And this menace is equivalent to demanding that an author shall take men and women at their own valuation, and ignore the hidden motives and forces which control human conduct. A very few strokes of the pen, a little falsification in character-drawing, and "Misalliance" could have been made an acceptable play; but there was a writer holding the pen who was inexorable. Mr. Shaw drew life as he saw it, and left the public to approve or not as it liked. But if London rejected "Misalliance," this did not kill the play; it is no more dead than Mozart's "Le Nozze di Figaro" is dead because on its first appearance Vienna sneered at the work of one whose talent outshone that of its own musicians. The Viennese winced and got over their dislike; in the same way Londoners will come to think well of "Misalliance." It is true that we are indebted to its author for at least one popular success, which future historians of the stage will declare was an epoch-making play, being the first of its kind to arrest the attention of the man-in-the-street, and bring him into the theatre to listen to nothing more exciting than a "talk." But the success of "John Bull's Other Island," so far as the public was concerned, had less to do with the merits of the play than the demerits of the audience. The City man woke up one morning to find himself famous, as he thought, and hugely enjoyed his notoriety. What did it matter if a company promoter was silly and cunning so long as he was always amusing and successful! This, as they thought, was the profound wisdom that Mr. Shaw meant to preach to the world! What a strange instance of egotistical vanity! And when the same play was performed in Dublin, the enjoyment of the audience was no less marked, but with this difference—that the laughter was all against Broadbent and not with him. Whether the Englishman was successful or not, he was a "fathead," because no Irishman was silly enough to put his pocket before his politics or to prefer his neighbour's omniscience to his own. Yet this play is not the less virile and wholesome because company-promoters think themselves flattered by it. It is not Mr. Shaw pandering to his audience, but vanity looking at itself in the looking-glass.

Of that other "failure," "The Madras House," Mr. Archer admits that he found a good deal in the play to interest him, and it is difficult to believe that the author of "The Voysey Inheritance" had not something fresh and inspiring to tell his audience. There are some subjects which do not admit of being treated in drama in a way to enlist general favour. No thinker would argue that "Troilus and Cressida" was written by Shakespeare with a

view to its surpassing the popularity of "Hamlet."
It is sufficient if the author has treated his subject
in a way consistent with the laws of nature and
probability. For the critics to assume, as they do,
that the author is not conscious of the dramatic
limitations imposed upon him by the choice of his
subject is an impertinence. As Voltaire once said
in defence of a play: "We cannot do all that our
friends advise. There are such things as necessary
faults. To cure a humpbacked man of his hump we
should have to take his life. My child is humpbacked, but otherwise it is quite well." Indeed,
Mr. Barker's time will be better employed in educating his critics than in re-writing his play. Nor
must it be forgotten that Mr. Barker was hardly out
of his teens when he wrote "The Marrying of Ann
Leete," a comedy that has not yet received the
attention it deserves. Fortunately it has been
printed and published, and will undoubtedly again
be seen on the stage; for the play has unusual
possibilities for a stage-manager with constructive
imagination and poetic sensibility, and there is not
now wanting in London an audience capable of
appreciating a work of the kind in the spirit in
which it is conceived. This comedy was undoubtedly inspired by the art of Maeterlinck at
the time when the Belgian dramatist was writing
such plays as "The Interlude." But where Maeterlinck fails Mr. Barker succeeds. With the poet the
disjointed dialogue and constant repetition of the
monosyllable becomes a mannerism, and is never
convincing. Mr. Barker's method is a nearer approach to reality. He has chosen his characters
with more care to give point to their abrupt method

of speech, and with no little art. In a country house remote from the world, among people who are well bred if not well read, who give more time to sport and cards than to books, and who have little power to express themselves except in unfinished sentences, is unfolded a domestic tragedy of wonderful power and sadness. And in this lies the weirdness and fascination of the play—that no word of the story is related by the characters, and only from fragments of conversation, apparently trivial and unimportant, does the spectator gradually bit by bit piece together and arrange for himself the puzzle of these people's existence. This comedy, then, is an experiment to try and show the inner life of a family exactly as it might be learnt by a neighbour who was not personally known to any of its members, and it is a very remarkable achievement.

To sum up. Let us be honest with ourselves and to others over this question of the Repertory Theatre, and drop the business side of the matter, which is not the vital one. Let us admit that we can easier spare from the ranks of our dramatists men like Barrie and Maugham than Shaw and Barker; for while the former seek to amuse us (for which we are grateful), the latter hold forth a hand to help us out of the ditch. Nor is it better for us to laugh with Messrs. Barrie and Maugham than to accept the proffered hand, leap out, and walk forward with the preachers.

THE ELIZABETHAN STAGE SOCIETY.

The Elizabethan Stage Society was founded with the object of reviving the masterpieces of the Elizabethan drama upon the stage for which they were written, so as to represent them as nearly as possible under the conditions existing at the time of their first production—that is to say, with only those stage appliances and accessories which were usually employed during the Elizabethan period. "Everything," said Sir Walter Scott, "beyond correct costume and theatrical decorum" is foreign to the "legitimate purposes of the drama," and it is on this principle that the work of the Society is based.

Although the actual life of the Elizabethan Stage Society began in 1895 it may be said to have had its origin as far back as 1881, when a performance of the first quarto of "Hamlet" was given in St. George's Hall, London, in Elizabethan costume, and without scenery. The play was acted continuously, and lasted two hours. Here, then, probably for the first time since Shakespeare's day, was reality given to Shakespeare's words: "The two hours' traffic of our stage." The success of this performance fully justified the experiment. It was generally admitted by those present that the absence of scenery did not lessen the interest, and that with undivided attention being given to the play and to the acting, a fuller appreciation and keener enjoyment of Shakespeare's tragedy became possible.

This performance was followed by others of a similar nature, and with the same results, and the advantage of representing the Elizabethan drama under the conditions it was written to fulfil being thus demonstrated, the idea was suggested of building a stage after the Elizabethan model, yet it was not until 1893 that this long cherished scheme was carried into effect. In the autumn of that year the interior of the Royalty Theatre, Soho, was converted into as near a resemblance of the old Fortune Playhouse as was possible in a roofed theatre. The play acted was "Measure for Measure," and in commenting upon this revival the *Times* said: "The experiment proved at least that scenic accessories are by no means as indispensable to the enjoyment of a play as the manager supposes"; and a professor of literature at one of our London colleges wrote: "I don't think I was ever more interested—nay, fascinated—by a play upon the stage, and now I shall ever think the cutting up into scenes and acts a useless cruelty and an utter spoiling of the story." A regularly constituted society was now formed, and among the first to subscribe were Mr. and Mrs. Edmund Gosse, Sir Walter Besant, Rev. Stopford A. Brooke, Com. Walter Crane, Professor Israel Gollancz, Professor Hales, Sir Sidney Lee, W. H. Thornycroft, Esq., R.A., Miss Swanwick, the Hon. Lionel Tollemache, and Lady Ritchie. At the performance of "Twelfth Night" at the Middle Temple in 1897 His Majesty King Edward, then Prince of Wales, was present as a Bencher of the Inn.

At the annual meeting of the Society in 1899, Sir Sidney Lee, the Chairman, said: "Speaking as one who has studied the works of Shakespeare and his contemporaries with some attention, both on and off the stage, I have never witnessed the simple, unpretentious representation of a great play by this Society without realizing more of the dramatic spirit and intention than I found it possible to realize when reading it in the study."

Of the Society's more recent revivals, the interest

aroused by the old morality play, "Everyman," both in London and in many towns throughout the country, and in America, was very marked. The last play given by the Society under the present direction was "Troilus and Cressida."

LIST OF THE SOCIETY'S PERFORMANCES.

1893. "Measure for Measure" - Royalty Theatre, London.
1895. "Twelfth Night" - - Burlington Hall.
 „ "Comedy of Errors" - - Gray's Inn Hall.
1896. Marlowe's "Doctor Faustus" St. George's Hall.
 „ "Two Gentlemen of Verona" Merchant Taylors' Hall.
1897. "Twelfth Night" - - Middle Temple Hall.
 „ Scenes from "Arden of Feversham" and "Edward III." - - - St. George's Hall.
 „ "Tempest" - - - Egyptian Hall, Mansion House.
 „   „ - - - Goldsmiths' Hall.
1898. Beaumont and Fletcher's "Coxcomb" - - - Inner Temple Hall.
 „ Middleton and Rowley's "Spanish Gipsy" - - St. George's Hall.
 „ Ford's "Broken Heart" - St. George's Hall.
 „ Ben Jonson's "Sad Shepherd" - - - - Courtyard, Fulham Palace.
 „ "Merchant of Venice" - St. George's Hall.
1899. Ben Jonson's "Alchemyst" - Apothecaries' Hall.
 „ Swinburne's "Locrine" - St. George's Hall.
 „ Calderon's "Life's a Dream" St. George's Hall.
   (Edward Fitzgerald's translation)
 „ Kálidása's "Śakuntalá" - Botanical Gardens.
   (Translated from the Sanscrit)
 „ "Richard II." - - - Lecture Theatre, University of London.
1900. Molière's "Don Juan" - Lincoln's Inn Hall.
   (Acted in English)
 „ "Hamlet" (First Quarto) - Carpenters' Hall.

1900.	Milton's "Samson Agonistes"	Lecture Theatre, Victoria and Albert Museum.
„	Schiller's "Wallenstein" - (Coleridge's translation)	Lecture Theatre, University of London.
„	Scott's "Marmion" - -	Lecture Theatre, University of London.
1901.	Morality Play "Everyman"	The Charterhouse, London.
„	"Henry V." - - -	Lecture Theatre, University of London.
1902.	Ben Jonson's "Alchemyst" -	Cambridge Summer Meeting.
1903.	"Twelfth Night" - -	Lecture Theatre, University of London.
„	Marlowe's "Edward II." -	Oxford Summer Meeting.
1904.	"Much Ado about Nothing"	London School Board Evening Schools.
1905.	"The First Franciscans" -	St. George's Hall.
„	"Romeo and Juliet" - -	Royalty Theatre, London.
1906.	"The Good Natur'd Man" -	Cambridge Summer Meeting.
1907.	"The Temptation of Agnes"	Coronet Theatre, London.
„	"The Merchant of Venice"	Fulham Theatre.
1908.	"Measure for Measure" -	Gaiety Theatre, Manchester.
„	„ „	Stratford-on-Avon Festival.
„	"The Bacchæ of Euripides" (Gilbert Murray's translation)	Court Theatre, London.
„	"Samson Agonistes" - - (Milton Tercentenary Celebration)	Lecture Theatre, Burlington Gardens.
„	Ditto	Owen's College, Manchester.
1909.	"Macbeth" - - - -	Fulham Theatre, London.
1910.	"Two Gentlemen of Verona"	His Majesty's Theatre.
„	„ „	Gaiety Theatre, Manchester.
1911.	"Jacob and Esau," and Scenes from "Edward III."	Little Theatre, London.
„	Schiller's "Wallenstein" -	Oxford Summer Meeting.
,	"The Alcestes of Euripides" (Francis Hubback's translation)	Imperial Institute.
1912.	Kálidása's "Śakuntalá" -	Cambridge Summer Meeting.
„	"Troilus and Cressida" -	The King's Hall, Covent Garden.
1913.	„ „ -	Stratford-on-Avon Festival.

SHAKESPEARE AT EARL'S COURT.*

The obsolete but picturesque phrase "Ye Olde" has perhaps something fascinating in it to the modern æsthetic temperament, but it would be just as well if those responsible for educating public opinion at Earl's Court about matters relating to the Elizabethan stage did not misapply the words. To the Elizabethan the Globe was a new building; there was nothing "olde" about it. What, then, the authorities mean is the Old Globe Playhouse, a definition that can mislead no one. There are some merits attached to the design, but also several errors, notably, on the stage, in the position of the traverse, in that of the staircases, and in the use made of the side boxes as approaches to the stage. These are details which are not of interest to the general public, and it is not necessary now to dwell upon them, though exception might be taken to the movement of the costumed figures who are supposed to impersonate the "groundlings."

The programme tells us that the vagaries of the groundlings are drawn from Dekker's "The Guls Horn - Booke," a satirical pamphlet published in Shakespeare's time, which can no more be seriously accepted as criticism than can a description in *Punch* of a modern theatrical performance. The evidence of foreigners visiting London in the seventeenth century gives a very different impression to that which Dekker chose to admit; and we are told of the staid and decorous attitude of those playgoers frequenting the Fortune, and of the stately dignity of the representations given at the Blackfriars. The handling of these incidents in the auditorium at Earl's Court have the appearance of being planned by one who is only superficially acquainted with the period and not in sympathy with the conditions of theatrical representation then in vogue—a circumstance to be regretted at an exhibition which was ostensibly organized to raise funds for a memorial to Shakespeare. Apparently it is forgotten that between 1590 and 1610 the finest dramatic literature which the world perhaps ever has known was being written in London, a co-incidence which is inconceivable were the staging so crude and unintelligent as that which is shown us at Earl's Court. Everything there appears to have been done on the assumption that 300 years ago there was a less amount of brain power existing among dramatists, actors, and audience than there is found among them to-day, while the reverse argument is nearer to the truth, for a Shakespearian performance at the Globe on Bankside was then a far more stimulating and intellectual achievement than it is on the modern stage to-day.

To illustrate this point it is only necessary to witness one of the "excerpts" presented at Earl's Court, the one called "The Tricking of Malvolio." Now, we may presume that attention is invited to the talents of the chief actor by the publicity given to his name, for on one small printed page it is "starred" five times in capital letters against the parts he impersonates. We can find no record of a similar keenness for publicity in any Elizabethan actor. But unfortunately this is the least remarkable illustration of modesty at Earl's Court, and it is impossible to suppose that so many mistakes could have been crammed into a single scene of "Twelfth Night" by anyone who had carefully read the play. Of Shakespeare's plays it was said, in his own day, that they erred from being too life-like, and that in consequence they lacked art ; that is to say, there was nothing theatrical about them. The persons he put on the stage, in their speech, costume, and manner, so exactly resembled those the audience recognized in the town that it was difficult to believe that the characters had not been transferred from the street to the stage. Now, in "Twelfth Night" the central figure in the story, and the one round which all the other characters revolve, is Olivia, a young lady who is plunged in the deepest grief by the loss, first of her father, and then of her only brother, and we are told that because of this grief—

> "The element itself, till seven years heat,
> Shall not behold her face at ample view ;
> But, like a cloistress, she will veiled walk
> And water once a day her chamber round
> With eye-offending brine."

We may presume, therefore, that, as in the custom of Elizabethan times, Olivia is dressed in the deepest mourning, and wears a black veil to hide her sorrowing face. Next in social importance, in Olivia's house, comes her uncle, Sir Toby, who, as a blood relation—for Olivia's father may have been his brother—also wears black, and, being a knight, should wear velvet or silk, and a gold order. He is out of humour with his niece for the way she parades her grief and shuts herself away from all company. To relieve the monotony of his existence he brings a fellow-knight into the house, calls back the clown who had run away out of sheer boredom, and gives himself up to eating, drinking, and singing. Maria, who marries Sir Toby at the end of the play, is a lady by birth and breeding, attending on the Countess, and, therefore, as one of the household, is dressed in black, and so also are the servants, including Fabian and Malvolio. These latter would all wear black cloth liveries, and Malvolio, in addition, a braided steward's gown, not unlike that worn by a beadle, with a badge on his arm showing his mistress's coat of arms, and a plated neck-chain, as a symbol of his office. It will be seen at once what a shock it would be to Olivia's sense of propriety, in view of her recent bereavement, for her steward to turn up unexpectedly in coloured stockings, especially when she had reason to believe that he had more regard and compassion for her sorrow than anyone else in the house, because of his staid and solemn demeanour. It is not unlikely, besides, that Malvolio, in anticipation of his certain promotion to the ranks of the aristocracy by his marriage with Olivia, had donned, in addition to yellow stockings, some rich costume, put on in imitation of those fashionable young noblemen at court who wore silk scarves crossed above and below the knee, since without the costume his own cross-gartering would not have been in keeping. And indeed in anticipation of his social advancement he alluded to this change of costume in his soliloquy, "sitting in my state . . . in my branched *velvet* gown." Here, then, was Malvolio appearing before the Countess in a "get up" that was not so much comic as audacious in its daring imitation of the only man suitable in rank to marry a rich countess—that is, an earl.

The environment, then, of the play is this: a house of mourning against which all its inmates are in rebellion with the exception of the Countess and Malvolio; the latter, who is a time-server, seizing his opportunity to ingratiate himself with his mistress by his pious and correct behaviour and the sternness with which he suppresses mirth within the house. All this information Shakespeare gives us in the text of the play, and yet how does the actor avail himself of this knowledge? Malvolio, the Countess's head flunkey, so to speak, appears not in the costume of a servant, but as if he were the best dressed person in the house. Had he been a peer of the realm and the Lord High Treasurer, his apparel, with one exception, could not have been more correct. Like Prince Hamlet, he is in black velvet, doublet, and trunks, and wears a magnificent black velvet gown reaching to his ankles, a gold chain and a gold order! Incongruous and impossible as this costume is for the character who has to wear it, an element of burlesque is added to it by the conical hat, a yard high, which never could have rested on any human head outside of a Drury Lane pantomime! Of course, when this initial error is made in the costume of the character impersonated by the leading actor, it is not surprising to find other mistakes made in regard to the costumes of those who appear on the scene. Sir Toby is not in black, nor does he wear his order of knighthood, but appears in a leather jerkin and stuffed breeches, as if he were an innkeeper! Not only is Maria not in black, but she is not even attired as one who is by birth a lady, attending on the Countess, since she wears the dress of a kitchen-maid; nor yet is

Fabian in black ; while the Countess herself appears
in a yellow dress, that being a colour Maria tells us
"she abhors," and without a veil, her face beaming
with smiles, as if she were the happiest creature in
the comedy ! What would any modern author say
if such liberties were taken with his play ? But
equally unintelligent is the reading of the text. For
Malvolio to say that when he is Olivia's husband
he will ask for his kinsman "Toby," is to miss
the humour of the situation. It is the pleasure of
being able to call Sir Toby a "kinsman" that is
flattering to Malvolio's vanity ; while in the same
scene the one word in Olivia's letter (of Maria's
composition) which is captivating and convincing
to Malvolio's credulity is unnoticed by the actor.
Malvolio's doubts as to whom the letter is written
are entirely set at rest when he comes to the words,
"let me see thee a *steward* still." From the moment
he gets sight of the word "steward," everything becomes as clear as daylight to him, so that when he
appears in his velvet suit before Olivia, and cross-
gartered—which does not mean the cross-gartering
of the brigand in Italian Opera, as the impersonator
imagines—his assurance carries everything before
him, and makes him turn every remark of the
Countess to his own advantage, and this self-
deception is kept up with unflagging animation,
until he flings his final words at his tormentors :
"Go, hang yourselves *all !* You are idle, *shallow*
things: *I* am not of *your* element ; you shall know
more hereafter." But this rendering of the scene
entirely misses fire at Earl's Court.

It would be ungracious and invidious, under the
circumstances, to indulge in criticism of this kind

without examining into the origin of the errors we have tried to point out. They are nearly all traditional. The actor is not the real culprit. If one appealed to him for an explanation, his answer would be, " What is good enough for Sir Herbert Tree is good enough for me," and Sir Herbert Tree might say, " What was good enough for Macready satisfies me." In the production of Shakespeare on the modern stage our actor-managers show originality and novelty. In the interpretation of Shakespeare's characters, and in the intelligent reading of his text, there seems to be no progress made and no individuality shown. In these matters we are still in the middle of the eighteenth century, the most artificial age in the history of Shakespearian drama. As a consequence, Shakespeare's plays are not taken seriously by actors of to-day. To them his characters are theatrical types which are not supposed to conform to the conditions that govern human beings in everyday life. They do not recognize that Shakespeare's art and his characters were as true to the life of his day as is the art of Shaw or Galsworthy to our own. Yet because the construction of his play is unsuited to the modern stage, therefore it is contended that Shakespeare is a bad constructor of plays, and any liberties may be taken in the matter of reconstruction that are convenient to the producer. And because his plays are written in verse, a medium we do not now use in modern drama, therefore it may be spoken in a way no human being ever did or could speak his thoughts. So it comes that there is always an apology on the actor's lips for " Shakespeare's shortcomings " whenever the actor wants to take liberties with this author. It is Shakespeare who is always in the wrong, and never the actor. Ask the actress who impersonates Olivia why she is not wearing a black dress, and she replies without a moment's hesitation that black is not becoming to her, as if it were an impertinence on Shakespeare's part to expect her to wear black. The havoc that is made with the characterization and story is of no consequence. "Oh, hang Shakespeare!" was what a popular Shakespearian actor once said to the present writer. That is the normal feeling of many actors towards Shakespeare's plays, and one which will continue unless public opinion can be roused to a sense of its responsibilities and insists that a more reverent and loyal treatment shall be bestowed on the work of the world's greatest poet and dramatist.

Unpleasant and ungracious as these remarks may appear to those who look to the Earl's Court Exhibition as a means for raising money for a national theatre, they are not unnecessary. From all parts of the country visitors, comprising many teachers and their scholars, come to this exhibition expecting to receive a correct impression of Shakespeare's playhouse and of the Elizabethan method of staging plays. But what they see cannot inspire them with confidence or belief that dramatic art at that time, both in its composition and expression, was at its high-water mark. This is because the spirit and the intellect of Elizabethan times are wanting. These qualities do not appear in modern actors nor in their productions. There is nothing to be seen but the restlessness of our own stage-methods, which no more fit the Elizabethan stage than would the Elizabethan methods fit the modern stage. In another of the excerpts given at Earl's Court, which is entitled the "Enchantment of Titania," the costumes, business, and action of the proscenium stage are wholly reproduced on the open platform. In Shakespeare's time the actors did not scamper all over the stage and in and out of the private boxes while they were saying their lines, nor was music played during their speeches. Then, again, the stage-management of the scenes from "The Merchant of Venice" in the poverty and meanness of their appointments and costumes is a libel on the old Globe representation. It is only necessary to consult the stage-directions in the first folio to recognize the fact. Bassanio then came on to the stage dressed like one of the Queen's noblemen, with three or four servants. At Earl's Court he comes on unattended in a pair of patched leather boots and worn suit, looking more like a bandit than a nobleman. There is no indication given of his superior rank to which so much importance was attached in Shakespeare's time. Indeed, those who are anxious to revive an interest in Elizabethan staging, and who urge its claim for recognition, are justified in making their protest against this travesty of Shakespearian drama.

A STUDENTS' THEATRE.*

1. *Miss Rosina Filippi's Project.*

This project, advocated by one who is herself an able exponent of dramatic art, both as an actress and a teacher, is worthy of careful consideration,

* *The Nation,* August, 1912.

nor can Miss Filippi's strictures on actors and managers be read with indifference or passed over in silence. It is asserted that acting is no longer a profession, but a business, and that it will continue to be a business until the actors themselves take the necessary steps to give their calling the status of a profession. This is true, because even if the public can be roused to demand that acting shall be treated as an art, it cannot manufacture artists, nor control the choice of the talent which is submitted to its judgment. Miss Filippi believes, moreover, that the thinking portion of the British playgoer is beginning to learn that English theatres need "something" before they can rank in reputation with those on the Continent, an assumption which cannot be denied; although Miss Filippi will hardly expect that all well-wishers of the drama will agree with her as to what that "something" should be. In this, indeed, lies the difficulty, for the divergence of opinion among actors on questions connected with dramatic art is so bewildering that both the public and the profession become indifferent to the controversy from mere weariness.

The question for consideration at the moment is the "Students' Theatre," and whether Miss Filippi's project is one more practical and more promising than the many rival suggestions now claiming attention and support from the public; and here, at least, there is room for criticism. In the first place, it may be doubted how far the public would support the theatre by buying stalls, even at the reduced price of 4s., in order to see students act plays which can be seen acted elsewhere under more favourable conditions. Let a novice be ever so well coached, yet the ordeal of facing a theatre full of human beings who all stare at him from the auditory deprives him of the power to control and move that audience. This is a drawback which can only be removed by long practice. Then, as a rule, youth possesses too eager and confident a temperament to appreciate the meaning of restraint. Students must wonder what chances they get by acting in a theatre where no reputations are allowed to be made, no personal ambition can be gratified, and no names may be inserted in the programme! And after reading about these severe impositions, which are to give artistic stability to the "Students' Theatre," it is a comfort to be told by Miss Filippi that it is not her intention "to serve the interests of any particular set of faddists, but to present good plays by a picked company of young actors." Let us hope, then, that Miss Filippi does not intend to limit her players to those who are students in the ordinary sense of the word. And, indeed, might not the co-operation be obtained of those artists who, being temporarily out of an engagement, would be willing to join Miss Filippi's enterprise in support of the cause she advocates, which is, in effect, a devotion to art for art's sake, and the still more praiseworthy desire to obtain for the art of acting some public recognition of what constitutes the standard of excellence? Such a combination of forces, under artistic control, would have far-reaching results.

And, after all, it should be possible for those actors who claim to take their art seriously to agree upon a certain standard of qualification which should be considered indispensable to everyone wishing to become an actor. The late Sir Henry Irving in a speech once said: "I think there is but one way to act, and that is by impersonation. We hear the expression 'character-acting.' I maintain that all acting is character-acting—at any rate, it ought to be." But we live in an age when personality is valued by the public at 50 per cent. more than is the talent of impersonation. As a consequence, it becomes more and more the practice among managers and dramatic authors to select actors for parts for which they are naturally fitted by age, face, voice, and temperament, with the result that the character is played by one who succeeds tolerably well, and even may excel in certain scenes, in the only part in which he is ever likely to excel. Yet such a one is not an actor at all in the legitimate sense of the word, and if he is without vocal or physical flexibility, he is limited to the business of impersonating his own personality. Then if he happens to appear in a play which becomes a success, he may hope to continue acting his own personality throughout the English-speaking towns of the two hemispheres for a run of four, or even seven, years, after which he will have the pleasure of "resting" until another part can be found for him as much like himself as was the last one. And while this method of casting plays has the advantage of distributing more equally the chances of an engagement in a profession which has always a larger supply of actors than is required, it has the distinct disadvantage of depriving the character actor of the opportunity of learning his art.

Now, it is evident that Miss Filippi's object in forming her "Students' Theatre" comes very near in its aim to the one the character-actors should have in view, that of removing the attention of playgoers from personality, and concentrating it on the art of impersonation. And this is an art which no novice can hope to excel in. The training for this kind of art requires a long apprenticeship, and the actor cannot hope to reach the topmost height as an impersonator until he has had many years of experience on the boards. In fact, he will have passed into the meridian of life before he can become a fine character-actor. May it not, then, be put forth as a practical proposition that Miss Filippi and her youthful enthusiasts should join forces with the charactor-actors, and try to run a theatre with some small public endowment for a common cause ? In this way there would be a possibility of the public being attracted, and willing to pay for its seats, having the assurance that both talent and experience would be seen at the " Students' Theatre."

The initial difficulty in such a scheme would, of course, be the admission of candidates, whether students or actors. And while it would be essential to ask for the willing co-operation of those actors who already possessed undoubted reputations as character-actors, a test qualification would have to be found which would inspire confidence both in the public and in the profession, that those who were elected members had in them the necessary material for the art of impersonating character. In fact, the reputation of the theatre should be built upon the knowledge that only those who had passed the test qualification were admitted to the rights of membership. The following kind of test might be tried, perhaps, to ascertain the ability of the candidate as an impersonator. He might appear before twelve of the members, and during the space of half an hour, without leaving the platform, impersonate three different characters all of the same type. If the candidate wishes to qualify for juvenile parts, then he must satisfy his judges that he is able to impersonate three young men who may have some resemblance to each other in appearance, but who are all different in character, in voice, and in deportment, or he may decide to be judged by his impersonation of middle-aged city clerks, bumpkins, or pedants; but in every case he should be able to satisfy his judges that he can show three distinct characters of the same type. In this way mere vocal dexterity, mimicry, and "make-up," would not insure election. The best character-acting is, of necessity, limited in its extent. The "light" comedian cannot and should not appear as the "heavy" father, nor the lean beggar as the fat boy. Some actors can include a larger range of parts in their repertory than others. But the real test of character-acting is in having the ability to reproduce subtle shades of characterization in certain recognized types.

In putting forth this plea for an enlargement of the scope of the proposed "Students' Theatre" it is hoped that, by some such suggestion, the difficulties in raising the necessary funds for the endowment which Miss Filippi at present experiences, may disappear. There is no doubt that the money would be forthcoming as soon as the public had a scheme presented to it which was the "something" needed. And the profession, on its side, should remember that, while it has established many associations to protect its business interests, it has not yet thought it worth while to devote either time or money to the by no means unnecessary part of a professional career, which shall provide actors with the opportunity of perfecting themselves in the study of their art.

2. *Mr. Gordon Craig's Sketches.*

Shakespeare has long since failed to hold his own against modern staging, and the possibility of bringing more taste, skill, and naturalness into the art of the scene-painter does not remove the difficulty, but rather increases it. When a dramatist is not on the spot to rewrite his play to suit the altered conditions of mounting, the question then arises as to whether the play or the scenery is the thing of most value. Mr. Sargent does not ask leave to repaint Raphael's canvas because the draperies in which the Italian artist has clothed his divine figures are conventional ones. The advocates for modernism demand that new wine shall be put into old bottles. No doubt there are some old stone jars that will bear the strain, in the same way as there are some old plays which will stand a good deal of decoration ; but the business of the producer is to know what kind of decoration is becoming to the art of the dramatist, and what is derogatory to it. Mr. Craig's art may help us to derive additional pleasure from the theatre, but will it help us to understand Shakespeare's tragedies ? If not, let him make his experiments on the plays of some less gifted dramatist. The inappropriateness of scenery for Shakespeare lies, mainly, in its unreality, and Mr. Craig tries to make it still more unreal. Such properties, or scenes, as were in use in the poet's lifetime were suggestive of immediate, and not remote, objects, because what is distant in place and time has less actuality than what is near at hand. To see in an Elizabethan playhouse built-up doors, windows, caverns, arbours, ramparts, ladders, prepared the minds of the audience for action, and brought the actors into closer touch with life.

Now, Mr. Craig's art resembles that of Turner. He has a sense of beauty and restraint, with a poet's insight into the meaning of landscape and atmosphere which stamps him as an artist, and distinguishes him at once from the scene-painter of Globe Alley. With him, as with Turner, it is the sun that is the centre of the universe. His passion is for airy landscape, unsullied by the presence of the concrete; and Turner's palaces, boats, and men seem shadowy things beside the splendour of Turner's sunshine. But the central interest of drama is human, and it is necessary that the figures on the stage should appear larger than the background, or let the readers of Shakespeare remain at home. To see Mr. Craig's "rectangular masses illuminated by a diagonal light" while the poet's characters walk in a darkened foreground, is not, I venture to think, to enjoy the "art of the theatre." There must be some sane playgoers who still wish to see in the playhouse Juliet smile upon Romeo, and Othello frown on Iago. "What a piece of work is man!" says the poet; but there is no room for man in Mr. Craig's world.

It is because Mr. Craig's art exposes to view a background which is effective and suggestive apart from the needs of drama, that it fails in its purpose. Had he studied the methods of Rembrandt, instead of those of Turner, something practical for the stage might have been forthcoming. With Rembrandt, whether

it is a windmill, a temple, or a man, it is always
the object, not the landscape, that arrests attention.
The light coming from the front, and not from the
side, first illuminates the objects before reaching the
background. The spectator, as it were, turns on a
bull's-eye lantern, and is thus able to see the story
written on the men's faces. Then the artist contrives
that the mind shall pass by an easy transition from
the faces to the more sombre background. But
unless this transition is gradual and the background
is sombre, interest in figures is proportionally
weakened.

Now, Mr. Roger Fry's sympathetic appreciation
of Mr. Gordon Craig's designs for " Macbeth " may
predispose his readers to believe that they form
a suitable background for a representation of Shakespeare's tragedy. Some years ago I saw Mr. Craig's
production of " Acis and Galatea," followed by a
masque. It was a stagery of great beauty, and
seemed to initiate new possibilities. But then both
were musical entertainments which gained ap-
preciably by a picturesque background. The action
never clashed with the quaint setting. Unlike the
demands of tragedy, the representation made no
direct appeal to the reason, and no obvious attempt
to purify the emotions. Its main business was to
delight the eye.

Mr. Craig, in his foreword to the printed catalogue
of his exhibition at the Leicester Galleries, remarks
that the designs and models " speak for themselves."
This admission is a merit if the designs are intended
for book illustrations. A picture which arrests the
attention and stirs the imagination gives a pleasurable

and legitimate emotion when it does not clash with the emotions aroused by the poet or the actor. Mr. Fry tries to answer this criticism, but not altogether successfully, since it must be remembered that Shakespeare, in his day, had no other way of approaching his audience except through the actors, and so he was obliged to construct his plays with this means in view. It is only necessary to quote from Mr. Craig's notes to his sketches to show that the poet and the designer do not always pull together, and that it is doubtful if Mr. Craig's scenery is more appropriate than any other kind of scenery when it is used as a background for a Shakespearian play.

" No. 2.—The aim of the designer has been to conceive some background which would not offend whilst these lines were being spoken."

But eight lines further on Macbeth says : " Liar and slave !" This arouses quite another kind of emotion from that of " To-morrow and to-morrow," etc., and one for which Mr. Craig's scene is not suitable.

" No. 3.— . . . So I conducted the lady to her bedroom, which is hung with red, and altogether a mysterious room, the only fresh thing being the sunlight which comes in. . . ."

There are three movements in this scene which stir varying emotions. The entrance of the lady with the letter, the return of the husband, the arriving of Duncan. The last two incidents are more dramatic than the first one ; but Mr. Craig never allows the spectator to forget the bed, the window, the light, and the letter. By the way, is it not moonlight which comes in at the window ?

" No. 11.—This is known as the ' Murder Scene.' I hope it is vast enough. . . ."

It is not the vastness of the scene, nor the huge door leading to the little room where Duncan lies murdered, which can show the terror in Macbeth's soul at the thought of what he has done, and this terror is the central idea of the scene.

"No. 16.— . . . As it is there is great need for scenery, and therefore the better the scenery the better for the play. . . ."

These words might be interpreted thus: "The more of Gordon Craig's scenery the better, because Shakespeare and his actors are very little good without it." But this is not at all what a producer should say.

" . . . Her progress is a curve; she seems to come from the past into the present and go away into the future. . . ."

Shakespeare makes Lady Macbeth come from her bedroom to speak a soliloquy about past events, and then sends her back to her bedroom. But Mr. Craig seeks to impose another idea upon the attention of the audience, which is not Shakespeare's idea at all.

"No. 17.— . . . As the sleeping woman descends the stairway with her lamp, she feels her way with her right hand, touching each figure, lighting them as she passes . . . and when she has gone from the scene all life has gone from the figures—once more they have become cold history. . . ."

A pretty idea, but absolutely at variance with the text. Shakespeare restates in this scene what led to the undoing of this unhappy but fascinating woman. Before the murder it was the material side of things only that appealed to Lady Macbeth. She thought it was as impossible for a murdered man to come out of his grave to torment his murderers as it was for a man who died a natural death. The dim consciousness that somehow she was mistaken begins to prove too great a strain for her energetic little brain. It was also her misfortune, because not her fault, that she was without imagination. She was a devoted wife, and possessed sweet and gracious manners; and Shakespeare, in this last scene, in which she appears before the spectators, asks them to pity her because of all that she is now suffering. But what has this throbbing emotion, aroused by the author, to do with these " dead kings and queens " in the cold statuary which has been superimposed by the artist ?

Mr. Gordon Craig seems to think that Shakespearian representation at the present moment is unsatisfactory, because of our miserable theatres, with their low proscenium and unimaginative scenery, which cannot suggest immensity ! Shakespeare would tell us that the fault lies in our big scenic stages and our voiceless, dreary acting ; and two men with such different ideas about the theatre are not likely to prove successful in collaboration.

The Memorial Scheme.*

" Doesn't that only prove how little important we regard the drama as being, and how little seriously we take it, if we won't even trouble ourselves to bring about decent civil conditions for its existence."—
HENRY JAMES.

Does the present scheme appeal to the nation ? Will it supply the higher needs of the nation's drama ? These are questions on which light should be thrown. Personally I should like to see every theatre in the country a national one, only the claims

* *The New Age,* June, 1911.

of the actor-manager and the syndicates stand in the way. Certain it is that the imagination of the public has not yet been touched by this Whitehall scheme; but then the executive committee has not made the best of its opportunity. It is two years and three months now since the first appeal for funds was made, and so far the response has not been encouraging. In March, 1909, the scheme was launched and priced at half a million of sovereigns; we are now within five years of April, 1916, and the total amount of money raised for the project is about £10,000, excluding the gift of £70,000 given by Sir Carl Meyer, and the amount raised by entertainments. Unfortunately, the cost of collecting this £10,000 has been very considerable, although it is not possible to quote the exact amount, because no accounts have been published during the three years the executive has been in office. In fact, the attitude adopted by the executive towards the general committee is what most calls for explanation.

HISTORY OF THE MOVEMENT.

The movement began so far back as the year 1900. It was then proposed by myself to present to the London County Council a petition for the grant of a site for the erection of a memorial in the form of the old Globe Playhouse, so as to perpetuate for the benefit of posterity the kind of stage with which Shakespeare was so long and intimately associated. The outcome of this proposal, which remained in abeyance during the anxious period of the war, was a meeting organized by T. Fairman Ordish, F.S.A., and held in the hall of Clifford's Inn on "Shakespeare Day," 1902. The chair was taken by Mr.

Frederic Harrison, and two resolutions were passed by the meeting, one establishing the London Shakespeare Commemoration League, the other recommending that the proposed memorial of the model Globe Playhouse should be considered by the committee of the League. It was ultimately found, however, that a structure of the kind could not be erected in a central position in London owing to the County Council's building restrictions. In the following year an interesting development arose in connection with the League in the formation of a provisional committee for a London Shakespeare Memorial. The movement was made possible by the generous gift of Mr. Richard Badger to the London County Council of the sum of £2,500 to form the nucleus of a fund for the erection of a statue, and the Council offered a site, if sufficient funds could be collected to insure a worthy memorial. The League then formed a provisional committee composed of a number of influential people, among whom were eight members of their own council, including the President, the late Dr. Furnivall. But the idea of a statue was not the only scheme offered for the provisional committee's deliberations. Some were in favour of a "Shakespeare Temple" to "serve the purposes of humane learning, much in the same way as Burlington House has served those of natural science." This suggestion, however, called forth a protest, and on February 27, 1905, a letter appeared in the *Times* in which it was stated that "any museum which could be formed in London would be a rubbish heap of trivialities." The letter was signed by J. M. Barrie, Professor A. C. Bradley, Lord Carlisle, Sir W. S. Gilbert, Mr. Edmund Gosse,

Mr. Maurice Hewlett, the Earl of Lytton, Dr. Gilbert Murray, Lord Onslow, Sir A. W. Pinero, Sir Frederick Pollock, Mr. A. B. Walkley, and Professor W. Aldis Wright. On the next day was held a public meeting at the Mansion House, with the Lord Mayor presiding. No special mention of a statue was made, nor of a "Shakespeare Temple," while Mr. Bram Stoker pointed out the difficulties and expense of a National Theatre. On the proposition of Dr. Furnivall, seconded by Sir H. Beerbohm Tree, the following resolution was passed:

> "That the meeting approves of the proposal for a Shakespeare Memorial in London, and appoints a general committee, to be further added to, for the purpose of organizing the movement and determining the form of a memorial."

On this general committee I was asked to serve and was duly elected.

On Thursday, July 6, 1905, the general committee was summoned to the Mansion House to receive the report of the special committee appointed to consider the various proposals. This committee, which was elected by the general committee, was as follows: Lord Alverstone, Lord Avebury, Lord Reay, Sir Henry Irving, Sir R. C. Jebb, Sir E. Maunde Thompson, Mr. F. R. Benson, Mr. S. H. Butcher, Mr. W. L. Courtney, Mr. Walter Crane, Dr. F. J. Furnivall, Sir G. L. Gomme, Mr. Anthony Hope Hawkins, Mr. Bram Stoker, Dr. A. W. Ward.

The recommendation made by this committee, which was unanimously adopted, was that "the form of the memorial be that of an architectural monument including a statue." But it was also recommended, if funds permitted, as a possible subsidiary project, "the erection of a building in which Shakespeare's plays could be acted without scenery." This part of the scheme met with strong opposition from some members of the general committee, and Sir Herbert Tree, as representing the dramatic profession, declared that he could not, and would not, countenance it.

Finally, by the narrow majority of one vote (that of the chairman, Lord Reay) it was decided that this part of the report should be dropped, as well as the proposal to use, as a site, a space near the new London County Hall, recommended for its proximity to the locality of the old Globe playhouse.

On March 5, 1908, the general committee were again summoned to the Mansion House to receive the further recommendations of the executive committee after their consultation with an advisory committee consisting of seven persons, five of whom were members of the Royal Academy. The meeting confirmed the recommendation that a statue be erected in Park Crescent, Portland Place, at a cost of not less than £100,000, and an additional £100,000, if collected, "to be administered by an international committee for the furtherance of Shakespearian aims." What was remarkable to me about this meeting was the small attendance. There could not have been more than two dozen persons present. I believe I was the only one there to raise a debate on the report, and, my objections being ignored, letters from me appeared the next day in the *Times* and the *Daily News* attacking the constitution of the committee selected to approve of the design. Among those chosen there was not one Shakespearian scholar, no poet, and no dramatist. What, then, would be the effect upon the designers of having to submit their models to a committee of this kind ? Instead of the artists giving their faculties full play to produce some original and great piece of sculpture worthy of Shakespeare's genius, they would be striving to design something specially suited to meet the limited and, perhaps, prejudiced ideas of their judges (the professional experts), while the general committee, responsible to the public for the National Memorial, would be handing over its duties to an academy which had never shown any special appreciation of the poet and his plays ; for, so far as my experience goes, there never has been a Shakespearian picture exhibited on the walls of the Royal Academy which was not, as to costume and in idea, a burlesque of the dramatist's intentions, always excepting those painted by Seymour Lucas, R.A., who, strange to say, was not one of the judges selected.

But it soon became evident from correspondence in the newspapers that the project of a statue in Portland Place did not satisfy the wishes of a very large number of influential men, and of a very important section of the public. Accordingly, a public meeting took place at the Lyceum Theatre, under the presidency of Lord Lytton, on Tuesday May 19, 1908, when a resolution was carried in favour of a National Theatre as a memorial to Shakespeare. Steps were then taken to amalgamate the existing Shakespeare Memorial Committee with the National Theatre Committee. A new executive was nominated, and again, for the third time, the general committee was summoned on March 23, 1909, to receive and sanction the report, which recommended the raising by subscription of £500,000 to build and endow a theatre in which Shakespeare's plays should be acted for at least one day in each week.

This, then, is the history of the movement, we may almost call it of the conflict, which for seven years centred round the great event that is to happen in 1916. And, alas! this scheme, like all the others, is now found to be impracticable, because the amount of money asked for is far more than the country is able to give. The executive did not grasp the fact that there is so large a demand made upon the public's purse to fight political battles and to fill the Government treasury, that half a million of money cannot now be raised both to build and endow a theatre. The executive is obsessed with the notion that you cannot have a National Theatre without building a new theatre, while as a fact you cannot have it without an endowment. It is by protecting the art of the actor, so that the poet's words and characters may be finely interpreted, that the memory of Shakespeare can be best honoured.

THE EXECUTIVE'S REPORT.

We now have to consider what seems to me to be the chief flaw in the National Theatre scheme as it is at present initiated, and that is the report which was brought before the general committee on March 23, 1909, and which was accepted by them, but not without protest — at least, from myself. The Lord Mayor's "parlour" was crowded with at least a hundred men and women, consisting of the general and provisional committees of the two rival schemes, now amalgamated, all of whom were meeting together for the first time; and it was evident to me that with the exception of the executive, those present had little idea of what they were called upon to do, or were aware that they were conferring powers upon the executive as to the management of our National Theatre which, when once granted, made it impossible for the general committee to reopen any point, to revise their decisions, or to alter them. It is true that the executive stated in their report "that the time had not arrived for framing statutes in a form which could be considered final," but so far as the general committee was concerned what they once sanctioned they could not withdraw. On the other hand, what modifications or additions the executive afterwards made in the report should naturally have come again before the general committee for its approval, a point overlooked or ignored by the executive, as will appear later on. But the fact is that the report is a mistake, and should never have been passed by the general committee, for it either states too much or too little, and can please nobody. Since the executive had decided that they must purchase a site and build a new theatre (an altogether unnecessary proceeding, in my opinion), it would have been better to report on this part of the scheme first, and to leave the question of management for future discussion; for the financial question alone might well have received more careful consideration. As the report now stands, subscribers are not protected in any way. The executive may begin building whenever they choose, and incur

debts, and mortgage both land and building as soon
as they possess either. They can spend on bricks
and mortar all the money they receive to the extent
of £250,000, without putting by a penny towards
the endowment fund. In fact, no precautions have
been taken to avoid a repetition of the disaster that
befell the building of the English Opera House,
which soon afterwards became the Palace Music-
Hall.

But more inexplicable still are the clauses referring
to the management of the theatre, to which, unfortunately, the general committee have pledged themselves. We have decided that "the supreme
controlling authority of the theatre" shall be a
body of governors who will number about forty,
but apparently their "supreme control" is limited
to nominating seven of their number as a standing
committee, some of whom, and under certain
eventualities all of whom, may be elected for life.
This standing committee, however, is to hand over
all that is vital in the management of a theatre to
a director over whom it has no control beyond
either confirming all he does or dismissing him, so
that the National Theatre in reality becomes a one-
man's hobby. So long as the director is clever
enough to humour four out of the seven members
of the standing committee, he can run the theatre for
the amusement of himself and his friends. He may
choose the plays, arrange the programmes, engage
and dismiss the artistes, and can even produce all
the plays himself; the only thing he cannot do is to
act in them; and yet so little have the framers of
the report grasped the realities of the situation that,
in their other clauses, they refer to the governors

dispensing pensions and honorary distinctions on the actors, forgetting that the unfortunate players are the servants of their servant the director, who can dismiss them three days before the honours and pensions become due, so that even in dispensing favours the voice of the director is supreme. As the report stands at present confirmed there is no elasticity allowed to the standing committee to give permanency to those parts of the director's management which are evidently successful and efficient, and to restrict and finally abolish what is unsatisfactory. There is no choice between dismissing the director, or tolerating his defects for the sake of what he does well. But the director should be the chairman of the standing committee; he should have power to engage the producers of the plays, because more than one is wanted; and each producer should be given sole control over the cast and the staging of the play for which he is specially engaged. Then in the case of failure there would be always a remedy. Producers, authors, and actors who showed that they were unskilful in the work they were called upon to do would not be again invited to help in the performances of the National Theatre; but in regard to those who had shown exceptional talent, steps would be taken to gradually add them to the permanent staff, while the fact that the director was chairman of the standing committee would add to the dignity and importance of the artistes' engagements, and would insure respect and fair treatment for their labours. As the position is now, no talent can come into the theatre except at the will of one person, who would occupy no higher post there than that of a salaried official. This means that outside talent, however admirable of its kind, would never be seen in our National Theatre if it is not to the liking of the director; and it may be taken for granted, as the clause now stands, that no artist would accept dismissal from the director without appealing to the standing committee, hoping to prejudice the director in its eyes, and thus to create friction between the standing committee and its director.

Now, in regard to the choice of new plays. Here the standing committee apparently has the final word, which, as a fact, has no real value attached to it, because all new plays have first to be reported upon (that is, recommended) by the director and the literary manager, and if a new play is chosen against the wishes of the director, its fate is none the less sealed, since he has sole control over the casting of the play and its production. But before a new play can be produced at the National Theatre it ought to be submitted to the opinion of the three parties interested in its production. Experts know that a dramatic success depends upon (1) the quality of the play, (2) the ability of the actors who interpret the play, (3) the intelligence or taste of the audience; therefore the play, to be fairly judged, should be read before a tribunal consisting of the director, two dramatists (who have contributed plays to the repertory), two of the theatre's leading actors, and two members of the standing committee. Authors would then know that their work would be judged by experts representing every department of the theatre.

Then there is the question of what plays, other than new ones, should be included in the repertory. Here, again, the choice rests with the director, and if his taste is not catholic, what confusion he will make of it! For instance, are such plays classical as "Still Waters Run Deep," "The Road to Ruin," and "Black-Eyed Susan"? In one sense I think they are, because they represent the best examples of types of English plays at a certain period. But some men might not think so. It is too large a question for one man to handle.

The fault, then, of the constitution of the National Theatre, as it is at present framed, is that all the direction of what is vital to the dignity and permanency of the institution is put under the control of one man, when no single person can possibly have the knowledge and experience to cover so large a variety of work. Discrimination has not been shown between what is required of a Repertory Theatre and a National Theatre. The former is purely an experimental theatre, where courage and freedom is an advantage in a director. We look upon him as the pioneer to revolutionize existing conventions which have had their day and lost their use. He is an innovator, and we forgive his failures for the sake of his successes. Far different is the position of the National Theatre. Its mission is not to make experiments, but to assimilate the talent which has already been tried and found deserving, and to rescue from oblivion good plays for the permanent use of the community. Besides, its proceedings must be carried on with decorum. It has State functions and duties to consider; it has all shades of political and religious differences to take into consideration. One mistake might alienate the support of Royalty or of the Government; of Parliament, of the Clergy, or of the Democracy. Surely the direction of such an institution can be more efficiently carried on by a committee than by an individual!

Now, I sympathize with a National Theatre as a memorial to Shakespeare, because I think the highest honour that can be rendered to our poet-dramatist is to provide English actors—and Shakespeare was himself an actor—with a permanent home where dramatic art as an art can be recognized and encouraged ; and a National Theatre can give dignity to the dramatic profession and inspire emulation among its members by conferring upon them honours and rewards, provided always that the actors are the servants of the institution and not of a salaried official in that institution.   Personally, I do not care to see Shakespeare acted in a modern theatre, and I do not think his plays can ever have justice done to them in such a building.   But, none the less, I look upon a National Theatre as an imperative need if the drama is to flourish, and I believe, if Shakespeare were living to-day, he would say so too. The executive of the present Memorial, to my mind, made a false start by concentrating public attention on the building as the primary object, instead of on the institution, and then by ignoring the claims of the dramatic profession to recognition.   The labour, the anxiety, the expense of providing the public with plays in this country has been hitherto, and is still, borne by our actor-managers.   They at present are the people's favourites, and all have individually a large public following.   It was but just to these men to ask them to come into the scheme as honorary members of the institution, in the hope that they would associate themselves with those parts and plays of more than ordinary merit which undoubtedly have a claim to be admitted into the repertory of a National Theatre, and with which they individually were specially identified.   But while I appreciate the wisdom and justice of inviting those gentlemen who have hitherto borne the burden of theatrical management to contribute the best of their talent to the stage of a National Theatre, I fail to see the advantage of their help on the executive. However eminent as an expert a man may be, his use on the executive entirely depends on the confidence he inspires among his fellow-councillors, and it is only necessary to read the names of those who constitute the executive to realize that there is no possibility of any one personality dominating the council. As a consequence, the committee breaks up into groups whose aims are more political than practical. The second urgent matter for consideration by the executive was the provincial Repertory Theatre. Where is the advantage of a National Theatre in London unless there are existing at least six Repertory Theatres in the provinces which may serve as training grounds for actors and for the experiments of dramatists? Every encouragement, then, should have been given to our leading municipalities to interest themselves in raising money to endow local Repertory Theatres, and the executive of the London Memorial would be doing more good to the cause of drama by spending the interest of its capital in helping these local theatres to come into existence than by wasting their money in the way they are doing at the present time. Indeed, it seems as if the only hope of a National Theatre becoming a reality will consist in the assurance that the capital already raised shall be set apart for the endowment fund, and that only the interest of this capital shall be available for expenditure by the executive committee.

INDEX